CAKES
AND
ALE for the
PAGAN
SOUL

CAKES AND ALE for the PAGAN SOUL

Spells, Recipes, and Reflections from Neopagan Elders and Teachers

EDITED BY PATRICIA TELESCO

THE CROSSING PRESS
Berkeley | Toronto

The Crossing Press
A Division of Ten Speed Press
P.O. Box 7123
Berkeley, California 94707
www.tenspeed.com

Distributed in Australia by Simon & Schuster Australia, in Canada
by Ten Speed Press Canada, in New Zealand by Southern Publishers Group,
in South Africa by Real Books, and in the United Kingdom
and Europe by Airlift Book Company.

Cover and interior design by Lisa Buckley

Excerpt on pages 82 through 87 previously published in
Witch Crafting: A Spiritual Guide to Making Magic by Phyllis Curott
(New York: Broadway Books, 2001).

Library of Congress Cataloging-in-Publication Data

Cakes and ale for the Pagan soul : spells, recipes, and reflections from
Neopagan elders and teachers / edited by Patricia Telesco.
  p. cm.
  ISBN-10:1-58091-164-1
  ISBN-13: 978-1-58091-164-1

  1. Neopaganism. I. Telesco, Patricia, 1960–
  BP605.N46C35 2005
  299'.94—dc22

                    2004026849

First printing, 2005
Printed in the United States of America

1 2 3 4 5 6 7 8 9 10 — 09 08 07 06 05

CONTENTS

COMMUNITY: HONOR, RESPECT, AND GRATITUDE

RITUALS FOR LIFE

HEALING, SPELLS, AND OTHER SUNDRIES

ACKNOWLEDGMENTS

With gratitude and respect for each of the elders, teachers, facilitators, and leaders who took time out of their very busy schedules to help make this book possible. Here, for a few minutes, readers have a chance to look into your world and know you as fellow human beings and spiritual seekers who are simply walking the road the best they can.

INTRODUCTION

Patricia Telesco

Call it a clan, call it a network, call it a tribe,
call it a family. Whatever you call it,
whoever you are, you need one.

—Jane Howard—

Everything old is new again. That's the saying, and it's certainly true when we examine Neopagan practices and the people who have led this revival. The last recorded execution of a Witch took place in Germany in 1775. It's not surprising, therefore, that historians note a quietness about Witchcraft until the nineteenth century. It was during this period that nature again came to be revered, especially in art. With this renewed vision of the Earth as a reflection of divine patterns and principles, it's not surprising that people also began talking about Witches in a new manner.

Witches were now regarded as a misunderstood group who deserved a second look. Well-known people like Sir Walter Scott rallied to their defense and began to speak about magickal methods as the pre-Christian techniques we know them to be. The public as a whole developed, along with a fashion for teatime divination, a curiosity about Witches and metaphysics, which in turn spurred the development of various mystical orders, including OTO (Ordo Templi Orientalis), the Golden Dawn, and the Rosicrucians. We can thank many of these groups for preserving the older herbal formulas, kabbalistic writings, and various types of high and low magick from around the world.

Throughout the 1900s, interest in metaphysical practices waxed and waned with the times and circumstances. It's safe to say, however, that by the end of the hippie era the New Age movement was starting to hatch into Western consciousness. Whole new breeds of Witches and Pagans emerged, carrying briefcases instead of broomsticks and using computers instead of cauldrons.

Certainly some of the public at large wasn't quite ready for this new, improved Witch. In fact, some still have trouble accepting the Neopagan movement as anything more than a fad. Nonetheless, the romantic period of the 1800s seemed to continue to resonate for the metaphysical community. Rather than mystery and secrets, the entire movement began to step boldly out of the closet to stand as a viable religion or spiritual practice.

By the 1970s, Gardener's book (*Witchcraft Today*) was selling steadily. Dianic witches began taking their place with feminists, and Alex Sanders had founded the Alexandrian Tradition. Around the United States and Europe hundreds of groups, covens, and even gatherings were forming. Just ten years later, Starhawk wrote *The Spiral Dance,* and even more traditions were getting settled into the New Age scene.

Students of the movement estimate that by 1980 there were approximately 10,000 Witches in the world. There is no question this number influenced the 1990s, during which New Age publishing and marketing soared to new heights and began to make its mark. Needless to say, it also began attracting media attention.

If you were to do a search on Amazon.com for Wiccan titles, you'd find well over 2,000 titles dedicated to this subject. There are an additional 10,000 products (minimally) tied into the Wiccan, Neopagan, and metaphysical lifestyle. When you add to these figures an awareness that some books sell as many as 1,000 copies or more a month, you begin to see how quickly New Age ideals are growing. One Internet site, www.witchvox.com (considered the best of the metaphysical online informational sites), has nearly 50,000 Witches listed from around the world, and over 7,000 related websites. Don't stop there, however. Drop the word *Witchcraft* into your favorite search engine. I get 1,140,000 listings (which represents three times the number of listings from three years ago).

Among all those numbers, there exists a core of individuals who have given up a lot of personal time and energy to support the metaphysical community. It is thanks to these people that the New Age movement has not died, nor dwindled, but continued to grow in beauty. This book celebrates such individuals, wherever they may be. We thank you for your gifts. We thank you for paving the road with your sweat and tears. We thank you for being *you*.

It has been a while since we, the contributors to this book, wandered into our first Neopagan gathering, circle, or festival. It has been nearly as long since we picked up our first magickal book. At that moment, our sense of wonder at the possibilities Paganism offered, and at our community, was nearly impossible to verbalize. To see so many different people join together like a family—a tribe, if you will— and celebrate their diversity was not only a gift, but a blessing. To see so many celebrate the human spirit was likewise impressive, and it certainly changed our lives forever. It continues to change and challenge us daily.

Having walked this path for more years than we're willing to count, we now find ourselves standing in the proverbial spotlight of the Neopagan community as leaders, elders, facilitators, and teachers. While most of us neither asked to wear these shoes nor sought them out, we are honored to serve the metaphysical community. We do so with respect and gratitude, and with an intimate awareness of the responsibility each of those roles brings to our lives. It's in the spirit of honor and love that we open our hearts and souls to you by offering our hospitality—come, enter these pages and share some cakes and ale to soothe your soul and bring a welcome smile to your face. Or, to use a fun phrase, come sit for a spell!

Over the years various teachers, ranging from Dorothy Morrison and Margot Adler to myself and Jesse Wolf Hardin, have discussed the notion of gathering our favorite magickal menus, helpful hints, reflective stories, and community experiences under one cover (typically while rushing off to give a lecture!). The thought of working together on something fun and fulfilling was nothing short of intoxicating. You have no idea how often such opportunities slip by, but this time it didn't. Each of us has amassed an amazing amount of material from which to choose for this book. We're excited to bring to you here what each feels is most helpful and most meaningful, and you won't be wanting for variety: you'll hear about people's path to discovery, the power of love, the way community has transformed and changed individuals, the wonders of nature, and much, much more.

As you might have guessed, this isn't a how-to book per se. It's more like sitting around a campfire with more than forty people, many of whose names you have probably heard in passing somewhere. As the fire burns, each tells a story—of hope, of transformation, of love, of struggle and victory. Some choose instead to share recipes, insights, or poems. This is, in fact, our version of a bardic circle, where the songs are unique, just like the person sharing them. And as you listen and read, you get a look into our lives and specifically how the Neopagan community and experience have touched us in significant ways.

Certainly, you'll find here a lot of wonderful ideas, and even some activities to try. We want you to be able to "bring home" the energy of these stories in viable ways, but just telling you how to enact various spiritual processes isn't really the goal. Instead, we want you to get to know us, what inspires us, what has brought us down this road, and overall just enjoy our virtual company for a while. We hope that you seek out the writers of various stories—those who inspired you the most— and come to know their work in the community on a personal level. So sit back, relax, and make yourself comfortable. Join us for the warmth, light, and welcome companionship of our community hearth. Let's start where all good stories begin—at the beginning. In this case, it starts with what has brought us all here: our path.

THE PATH
OF BEAUTY

O UR SPIRITUAL PATH is one that is always
growing and evolving. It's touched by
people, by experience, by hope and fear, by
sounds and silences. It's one of the beauties of
Neopaganism that we allow our vision to grow
and change, to mature with the era and our
knowledge of the world. These stories reflect
that transformational beauty.

CHOOSING PATHS:
THE WITCH WITHIN

PATRICIA TELESCO

Discovering that Paganism in all its forms exists is rather like learning to walk all over again. All the things you thought were stone-hard truths somehow become fluid and malleable. Perhaps it's because of a certain stubborn mentality that I seemed determined to run headlong into this amazing spiritual experience. Perhaps I was just lucky!

I remember as a child spending hours on end guppy hunting, gathering raspberries, and singing to the trees. The guppies tolerated my splashing (which I suspect was simply an excuse to get cooled off on a hot summer day), the berry bushes were always abundant, and the trees never minded off-key notes. It's no wonder I'm a Pagan: it was imprinted in my soul. I just didn't know it yet.

The days of lingering in a wooded glen went by the wayside with teenage angst, followed by college, followed by jobs. The teenage angst worked itself out (for the most part) in the setting of a Pentecostal church (yes, I'm serious). College worked itself out with dating, studies, and the realization that I needed to think a little more seriously about this "God" person and what I did (or did not) believe about him/her/it.

Employment worked itself out via a move to Boston, Massachusetts, where I found myself in a one-room apartment furnished with more bugs than actual living space. Little did I know that this was where my world would change, and whole new possibilities would sprout like young grass in spring.

I began having odd experiences. Truth be told, I thought someone had slipped something in a drink. People's faces would melt away into other images—but *feel* the same. Touching old jewelry would bring up a jumble of mental pictures that held no meaning for me whatsoever. I was just about ready to check myself into a loony bin. Thankfully, another Witch stood ready to help.

A lovely lady I knew in the Society for Creative Anachronism (SCA), Lady D, listened attentively to my tale. She smiled and nodded in that disconcertingly knowing way, and asked, "When can you come for a visit? I think I can help you." My ears pricked up—she didn't think I was nuts! I replied by asking if this weekend was too soon (right then would have made me happier, but I didn't want to impose).

When I got to her home, I couldn't help but notice some rather eclectic decorations. She'd lived in Israel as a child, and the lingering signs of rich culture were impossible to miss. Among the treasures were pieces of jewelry. "Pick them up and tell me what you feel or see," she said, in a tone that implied she fully anticipated something was truly going to happen. I shrugged and went through some thirty or more pieces, one at a time. After the last one she smiled, patted my head, and said, "There there, you're just fine. . . . Let me teach you about energy."

Being a kabbalist all her life gave Lady D a great sense for this whole object-reading thing. She wasn't surprised by what I told her about the people changing either—like objects, people hold the energy of past lives, so the skill often overlaps. As she explained, I tried to understand. It *sounded* reasonable and went a long way toward explaining my current situation, but why me, and why now?

Of course, there were any number of reasons why the spiritual door could have swung open then. The only thing I didn't know is just how far it had opened—that is, until ghosts and people's spirit guides started appearing. If I thought I was antsy before, now I was downright

paranoid! Thankfully, once again, the Universe provided some wonderful people, including my current husband and the folks at Crystal Hill
Farm, to help me balance out all these different energies. Without their
friendship and guidance (especially for meditation and grounding), I'm
not sure I would have sorted things out on my own. After all, you still
can't find Wicca in the yellow pages!

At that juncture I had no idea what to call myself. All I knew was
that the unseen world was touching my here and now and transforming
me in ways I barely understood. The Universe, however, having a keen
sense of humor, was not about to be undone. I was soon to attend my
first open circle. As I watched and listened to the celebrants, it was like
the first glimmer of light when a dimmer switch moves from off to on:
nearly everything they said I had felt in my heart before that day. As so
many people have said before, it was like coming home.

That was only the beginning of my story, not the end of it. Nonetheless, the book might have never opened if people hadn't been present,
attentive, aware, and kind when I most needed it. To each and every one
of them I send my eternal thanks.

To those of you reading this book who are new to the path, I say
a special welcome. You're embarking on nothing less than a lifetime of
adventure. Keep your eyes on the horizon, and learn well the path on
which you walk (this keeps your head and heart in balance). Don't be
afraid to ask for help; don't be afraid to ask questions. Find someone
you trust, and let that little bit of community nurture your experience.

A spiritual diary

If you don't have one already, begin keeping a spiritual diary. Think back on when you first got interested in the Craft. Write down the people, places, and things that inspired you the most. Record the memorable moments that transformed your soul. As you do, think about the whys of your path up to this moment, instead of focusing so much on the how-tos (the whys are what truly define us and our spiritual progress). To help get you started writing in your Book of You, there are many activities, suggestions, and ideas planted throughout this book.

Then, once a year (perhaps on your birthday), look back on this Book of You—to see how much you've grown, and to be reminded of all the wonderful people who have helped with that transformation. Last but not least, remember to tell those people thank you. They may not remember the moment that altered your life, but the gesture will be greatly appreciated and treasured.

—Patricia Telesco—

CROSSROADS OF LIFE

REV. SELENA FOX

The meditative journey called Crossroads of Life can be used to aid life planning and decision making when contemplating two or more alternatives along the path of beauty. Use it to help better identify and consider concerns as well as hopes about possible courses of action. Allow the deep, thoughtful moment to connect you with wisdom and guidance from the Divine within.

Set aside at least half an hour for this multipart meditation. Make your journey in a quiet, solitary place free of distractions. Sit comfortably, with a pen and journal nearby. Create sacred space, such as by blessing the area with incense and casting a circle of light around you. Call on the Divine according to your own spiritual path. Ask for inner guidance and support.

Now bring to mind the choices before you. Give each of the choices a name and list these names in your journal. Select two or three choices to work with on this journey; also include an option that is "not yet known." Have your journal and pen within easy reach so that you can note experiences as you take each step on this journey. If you have many choices, consider doing this meditation on several occasions, exploring different sets of choices each time.

After making your selections, close your eyes and take several deep, long, slow breaths to center yourself. Imagine yourself standing at a crossroads. Behind you is your life's path up to this point. As you look before you at the crossroads, envision several gateways, each marked with the name of one of the choices you have selected, as well as one for the not yet known. Look at the gateways before you until one starts glowing to signal you to explore its path first.

Imagine the gateway opening and yourself going down that path to explore it as a possible route for you. Pay attention to what you notice and experience as you travel on this path. Note any physical sensations, feelings, thoughts, and symbols that come to you. After you have journeyed on this path for a time and gotten a sense of it, pause. Let a word or phrase emerge in your consciousness that is connected to the essence of this road as a possible life direction. Now, with this message in mind as well as your other impressions, turn around and return to the crossroads. Record your experiences in your journal.

After you have finished writing about the first path you explored, take some deep, slow breaths to center yourself and prepare for additional exploration. Imagine yourself again at the crossroads and scan the other choices until one of the gateways glows to signal you to try it next. Repeat the exploration process, including pausing and receiving a message. After you have returned to the crossroads again, note your experiences with this second path in your journal. Repeat this meditative exploration process until you have tried each of the roads, including the not yet known.

After concluding the Crossroads of Life meditation, sit quietly for a few moments. Next, review the notes in your journal for each of the paths you explored. Write down any additional thoughts and intuitions that come to you. Put your journal away, give thanks to the Divine, dismiss your circle, and bring closure to your journey and reflection process. Use this meditation in combination with intellectual and intuitive approaches, such as rational analysis, dreamwork, counseling, divination, and keeping a journal in order to make your decision.

FEAR'S SHIP

DOROTHY MORRISON

I'll never forget my first Pagan festival. The weather was crummy, the wood was wet, and the mosquitoes were awful. Even so, I reasoned on my first evening there, it really wasn't so bad. I was, after all, spending time with folks of a like mind. And wrapping that thought around me, I drifted happily off to sleep.

Of course, I wouldn't have been so happy had I known what the ancients had in store. In fact, I probably wouldn't have bothered to sleep at all. Just a few hours later, I was jolted awake by a series of earsplitting screams—the screams of an unattended child looking for her mother.

Not being the maternal type, I pulled the pillow over my head and waited for someone else to tend to the ruckus. But as luck would have it, no one did. The child just kept on screaming, and I was forced to deal with the mess whether I wanted to or not—and all without benefit of coffee.

Funny how kids don't really need much to be satisfied. A hug, a kiss, and a warm hand to hold was all it took to ease Emily's fears—and, of course, a stroll to the lake, where we conjured some of the most potent magick that ever existed, because of a child's trust and a Universe intent on teaching a lesson. The magick was so strong that Emily didn't even want to find her mother; together we fondly named it the Ship of Fear. Try this ritual the next time fear threatens to overwhelm you in your journeys.

1 walnut shell half
1 fallen leaf (light leaves like maple or sycamore work well)
1 small twig (4 to 5 inches will do)
  A bit of resin from a pine tree

Thread the twig through the leaf to form a sail, and attach the bottom of the twig to the inner center of the walnut shell with the resin. The result will resemble a makeshift sailboat.

Then conjure up all worries and blow them into the boat— this may take several breaths—saying something like

> Worries go along with woe
> As I will, it shall be so.

Once the boat is infused with all fears and worries, place it on a body of water and set it to sail, saying,

> Sail away with worries gray
> Leaving joy behind to play
> Only smiles are left for me
> As I will, so mote it be.

Turn around and leave, knowing that worries and fears have sailed far away.

FACING YOUR FEAR

BONNIE JEAN HAMILTON

The circle was cast amid glowing grins of jack-o'-lanterns as clouds of sage smoke silently drifted across the room. The area had been smudged and purified, along with each anxious participant. There were a few nervous newcomers, the old hands, and one Pagan child. This was the Unitarian Universalist Fellowship, a place where all religions come together in celebration of life. On this particular night, however, the Witches were in charge, leading the Samhain ritual on the thinnest of nights.

The quarters were called and the God and Goddess invoked. It was a time in the cycles of nature for the passing over of the Grain God. The celebrant enacting the role of the Goddess, in black flowing robes, circled around with her cast-iron lantern in the shape of an owl. It flickered and cast long shadows in all corners. The Grain God, waning in strength, gave his farewell and made his descent to the Underworld, which in this case lay beyond a cloth veil hung earlier in the night. There he would become the Dark God.

The Goddess, with love in her heart, invited each participant to walk the path leading to the Land of Apples, the Underworld. Once there, they would meet the Dark God to receive counsel and speak with their ancestors. The drumming began as the Goddess made an offering of an apple to the spirits. Sound traveled and reverberated off the vaulted ceiling, making three drums seem like many more, and all the people swayed and danced to the beating rhythm.

The flickering light led the way through the haze as the Goddess tenderly guided each soul, one by one, along the path. Men and women became entranced, moving freely and openly, without fear. Slowly they made their way to the Underworld, to meet the God and their ancestors. As they neared the gate, some suddenly became unsure, even frightened, as the Goddess led them to cross the veil and continue on their own. Some squeezed her hand in a plea for her not to let go, but the loving Goddess, being the supportive mother she is and knowing that all children need independence, smiled and gently pushed them forward. Freedom and lively dance seemed to turn to fear in grown men and women as they approached the unknown, looking back for reassurance from the Goddess, taking tiny steps forward toward the Dark God.

The Dark God, dressed in a black cloak with an antlered deer skull as his face, beckoned each one to join him at a special altar where the ancestors awaited communication. As each person approached, the Dark God said, "Once you pass beyond the veil, let all your fears disappear. This is not a place of fear and dread, but one of rest and solitude; a waiting point in your journey. Come forward, my child, and gaze into the mirror." Each participant had a different experience, and some were even moved to tears as the God guided them in contacting their loved ones. All were glad they had made the journey.

I was the Goddess that night, and it surprised me to find that many adults were hesitant to walk the path and afraid to enter the dark behind the veil. There was one, however, who did not falter—a Pagan child. She joyfully skipped her way around the circle and straight into the Land of the Dead to face the presiding God. She had no fear in her heart, and nothing to hide. I found merriment in this and gave a little laugh when she let go of my hand and didn't look back. The Goddess did not need to give this child a push; she had all the strength she needed by knowing herself and not being afraid.

Unfortunately, we don't all feel this freedom. We each have fears that hold us back, keeping us from following our paths and living our dreams. Our fears cause stagnation and sadness. Perhaps, when many of us were children, we felt free and full of life, excited about the years ahead. Who knew what was to come, and what possibilities we could grab hold of. There was no fear of failure, only hope. If we could recapture what we had then . . . but even if we didn't have it then, we can still find that freedom within ourselves.

releasing your fears

Take a few moments to imagine what it is that scares you most. This exercise isn't fun, but when performed diligently it can be quite effective. Whatever your fear may be, start by drawing a picture of it or something that symbolizes it for you. Place your drawing on an altar or in a special place and tell God and Goddess you no longer want to be controlled by your fear.

Whenever you walk by the altar, look at the picture and tell yourself that you are not afraid. The transformation may take some time and patience, but it will work if you have the willpower to make it happen. Be prepared to receive insight in various forms, such as from omens and dreams. Your desire to be free from the fear will work its way into all levels of your being and start to manifest in your life.

No matter what your fear is, you can face it head on. Many people fear spiders, so I will use them as an example. Spiders are just like you and me, trying to make their way through life, and they do not go around biting people for no reason. Try looking at spiders in a new way—as children of the Goddess who have their own mysterious ways but are sacred, just the same.

At the next dark moon, you may consider performing this ritual:

Create a sacred space for yourself that you will use later, at a time when you will not be disturbed, preferably at night. Include a small altar on which you may rest the drawing of your fear, essential oil of your choice, a lighter, and a small cauldron or large censer, along with your deity images and representations of the elements Earth, Air, Fire, and Water.

Take a relaxing bath to wash away any negativity and then enter the prepared sacred space. Cast a magick circle and call to the quarters and your patron deity. You may sit or stand, whatever makes you comfortable. Pick up your drawing and look at it, thinking about how it makes you feel. Let the fear build inside you until you cannot hold any more of it. Now, send that fear from within yourself into the drawing. Fill it completely with the fear that holds you back.

Cover the paper with essential oil and, placing it in the cauldron or censer, light it and let the fire spirits devour it. As the paper burns, ask your deity to take away what has held you back, removing all the fear within you. Feel the bad feelings float away, far away from you. See yourself being cleansed as the fear leaves your body. Your deity will take that energy to another place to be used in a more constructive fashion. You are free of it. Remember that the next time you see a spider—you have no fear!

When you are able to control your fears, many doors will open for you. Imagine what you can do when there is no fear to hold you back. I don't mean to say that you will never be frightened or scared; what I mean is that when you have control over your fear, it will never paralyze you or constrict your thoughts or behavior. You will be free to do those things you came into this life to accomplish. When you are not afraid, you will be able to feel your sense of self, which will boost your confidence and create happiness in your life. Once you have released one fear, you can work on others, one at a time, until you feel your soul shining through, allowing you to follow Spirit. Blessed Be!

—Bonnie Jean Hamilton—

INTIMACY WITH SELF AND OTHERS, EARTH AND SPIRIT

LOBA

In my work in the canyon where I live, at Sweet Medicine Sanctuary in New Mexico, the spirit of intimacy becomes apparent, be it with Earth or with our visitors. One careful step after another, the women who travel together here descend not only deeper into the canyon but deeper into the unexplored aspects of self and sisterhood, purpose, place, and their path. Together we wonder at the magic of the fairy grass, embrace and engage oak trees and ponderosa pines, and stare for long stretches at the mandalic patterns of lichen nested atop volcanic rocks. There are precious moments spent admiring shiny red beetles mating on stems of willow, acknowledging each lovely butterfly that flies by.

We say few words, speaking more in gestures and giggles, waved scarves, deeply drawn breaths and sighs. There is so much to notice and celebrate that we find ourselves drawn down into the present moment, with no thoughts of our troubles or traumas. It doesn't erase our histories, but it offers us a new chapter, creating a shared story of sisters connected through the umbilical of the Earth. We know ourselves as one, not through thought and conclusion but through touch and tears, laughter and love: through a deliberate process of coming closer.

Intimacy is conscious, intentional familiarity, requiring an investment of time, focus, and response, and it's something we all need along the path (with or without a canyon to help in pursuing that goal). The word derives from the Latin *intimus,* meaning "within." The path to greater familiarity with other people and other species begins by delving into our own inner reaches, by the processes of acknowledging and binding together the diverse parts of our whole and sacred selves. We hold the power to unify our seemingly disparate parts—our lust with our innate purity, our need to grieve with our need to celebrate, to feast as well as fast, our need to give love and attention as well as to receive these precious gifts. Intimacy is sharing aspects of our authentic selves, and to do that credibly we must first know who we are.

How precious is the time we invest in developing intimacy! Time with ourselves, taking every opportunity to be alone, offers a chance to get out of our heads and feel what is going on in our hearts. We make every quiet moment meaningful and do our best to banish the endless mental tape loops of self-analysis, criticism, fantasy, and projection that we so often lose ourselves in. We focus through our hearts. What are we really feeling? What unmet needs leave our hearts aching? It can be scary delving into the depths, because then we have to take responsibility. No wonder we distract ourselves with radio, television, magazines, when we have time that could be used for intimate prayer, for sacred solitude . . . or for sacred relationship.

Complete honesty, with ourselves or others, is absolutely essential for intimacy. Do we kid ourselves about our needs, fears, and unrealized dreams? Do we find ourselves relating to our friends through the superficial—talking about movies, sports, other places and times than the here and now? Or do we share our rawest wounds, our most precious dreams, our hugest fears, our inspirations and strengths? Do we speak only of ourselves, or do we ask others to share their hearts as well? True intimacy between humans requires a constant uncovering of the protective layers we build around us.

We too often get hurt, patronized, or criticized when we show our vulnerability. But to be real and open requires effort on all our parts, in every unfolding moment. If we have done the work of knowing ourselves, we can at least become conscious of whenever we allow a "mask" to assume our identity. Intimacy requires that we listen closely to our intuition and challenge each other whenever a loved one seems to be indulging in illusions and expecting us to reinforce a state of denial. Intimacy is almost always more of an effort than staying in the "shallow end" of things, and it is much aided by our clear vision and intention.

At the women's gatherings I facilitate, as much as I make space and time for wordless sharing, we also take in the blessing of medicine talks. It's amazing to hear the powerful stories that each woman carries. And it's even more amazing that no matter how different our stories are, there are common threads that bind us all together. We have all endured grief and heartbreak, experienced extraordinary transformations and powerful transitions, given huge amounts of love and energy to what we are passionate about, experienced bouts of disconnection and self-doubt, and had times blessed with grace and wonder. We laugh at each other's most improbable stories, and tears fall down our faces as we come to know each woman's heartbreak as our own.

It's important to make our conversation and contact as intimate as possible. Going for walks together in nature and agreeing to stay in the present moment helps. Candlelight, beautiful clothing, the perfect music, wood heat, smudges, and so on are all aids to creating an intimate space for our special times together. We can treat ourselves, as well as our dear friends, family, and lovers, to these intimate gestures, and in giving foot washes, massages, home-cooked meals, and decadent desserts we say, "This is how much I care about you!"

In the most healthy relationships we dish out both loving challenges and deep nurturing. Paying close attention to the needs of others at all times, we do whatever we can to help one another thrive. This is true whether we are talking about our sisters and sweethearts or the living Earth of which we are a part. We feel the pains and frustrations of others as we would our own, experience their ecstasies exploding in our hearts. Touching each other deeply, we are in turn touched. We know in our bodies the truth of our oneness, not only with our sisters but with all of creation.

Intimacy depends on an advanced degree of empathy, which can be a difficult load to bear sometimes. As we share in the bliss of butterflies and the ecstasy of the ocean, we also take in the pain of the pavement covering so much of our Mother's sacred body, her children starving, the agony of bulldozers ripping into her beauteous curves. Opening our hearts to the All is not something we can do selectively, and we cannot take in the light without feeling and dealing with the implications of the dark.

This canyon is a special place of power, the energies here making intimacy with and instruction from the land itself accessible to everyone who is present and focused. I invite each woman here to feel welcome to experience herself as "at home" as possible, to feel safe to take off all the masks she wears in order to fit in and be functional in society— to let herself become once again as a little girl, full of wonder, beauty, strength, and vulnerability. In our blessed time together, we become living embodiments of the wisdom of little girls, daring to be real, daring to be close—running barefoot down the elk trails by the river, climbing trees, and splashing naked in the water. Baring our skin to the touch of the Mother's waters, her stones, her grassy green belly, together we become one with the canyon, and each woman goes back inspired to new levels of relationship with her own beloved home. We each become priestesses of place, by loving and noticing, by committing our playful as well as prayerful attention, and by giving thanks.

Intimacy flourishes with gratitude, and in our every act and gesture we embody thankfulness for the food and fire, for shelter and clothing, for inspiration and beauty, for the moon, for the little birds that flutter about as we skip through our last day together in the canyon. We embody thankfulness for this deepened familiarity with our selves and one another, and for this world we rejoice in—investing our whole beings, our loving focus, our trust, our promise, our prayer. And then from that space, we carry that intimacy into our lives, give it to our moment-by-moment truth, empower our paths, and spread the blessing.

JOY AND PEACE

MAMA DOYI-ASTARTE

The best advice I can give to *any* spiritual seeker, any walker on the path, is this—concentrate on your energy work. Meditate and feel the power within yourself. Visualize a ball of energy or light in your center of gravity (the location is a little different for each person). Visualize that ball surrounding you and growing stronger and brighter. Here you are safe, you are protected, you are strong. Now send down roots of light from that ball of energy to keep it secure (you will feel somewhat heavier if you're doing this right).

To ground yourself further, meditate and go deep within yourself, imagining a vine growing from the base of your spine down through the floor and through the ground, and then through all the layers, down, down, down through the molten lava of the Earth's core. Next feel the energy surge back up through the lava, through the layers of earth, through the floor, and through you; then focus and project that energy out toward the moon like a cone of power. Connect to the moon and let the energy return back to you.

Once you have established this place of balance, energy work becomes much easier. Know what you want to talk to deity about; then concentrate, connect with deity, name your request, and visualize it going up into the sky and past the stars and around the moon and up to where the temple of your deity exists. Imagine yourself at a three-way crossroads beneath the moonlight in front of that temple with a tray of gifts for the deity. Lay down the tray, ask your deity if you can enter, and when the temple doors open, go in! You're being welcomed.

This is a sacred place. Show your respectfulness in a way that feels right, submit your request, and listen—really listen to the answer. This might take a while. After receiving your answer, thank your deity and leave the temple, then go back to the crossroads and see yourself returning to the Earth, by way of the sky; see the light of your essence return to your body. Then slowly, very slowly, open your eyes. If you do what the deity has told you, your request should be answered.

Ground, center, build energy, direct energy, connect with your deity, ask, listen, learn, and return. All are great lessons in connectivity work, energy work, vision work, and life skills—and they are the key to joy and inner peace, no matter where your path may lead.

THE GODDESS'S CALL TO SERVICE: SHE MOVES IN MYSTERIOUS WAYS

REV. ALICIA L. FOLBERTH/HALFWOLF

How can you come to know yourself? Never by thinking, always by doing. Try to do your duty, and you'll know right away what you amount to.

—Johann Wolfgang von Goethe—

I've watched many who are leading in the Pagan community find themselves, just as I do, in the role of elder simply because they have been practicing a few years longer than most. And for the most part, they don't have elders of their own to fall back on. My magickal generation has its own set of obstacles to overcome just as much as the last in the process of bringing the Old Religion into the future. For those who also have been called to service, I'm here to say never lose heart. You must know that you aren't alone in the work you must do—and the work must be done! It's just too important. Never give up.

The path of leadership isn't easy or kind. Those who lead are often forced to progress on the path more quickly. Considering that the Old Religion is already a path of deliberate growth, this is no quick-fix undertaking. You end up being challenged in ways that you never dreamed, and the personal work you must do to become an effective priest or priestess—to grow into the oversize shoes of leadership—is enormous. Leading in the community will shape you and temper your soul like a sword; you will be placed in the hot coals so that the raw steel of who you are can be forged. Every challenge is another blow to the metal, shaping you and making you stronger, until you find yourself very different from the person you were when you began. And you must grow if you wish to succeed; you simply have no choice, since the Universe will demand it of you.

It has been a very hard, long, and rocky road for me, having spiritually grown up in the Neopagan community. I've joked that running a temple is like the old slogan for the Peace Corps, "The toughest job you'll ever love." In part the difficulty came in having to grow up quickly on every level. There were many days when giving up seemed easier than going on, but something—typically Spirit—kept it from happening. The deities move in mysterious ways. Look for and pay attention to their signs and they will show you what you need to know and what you need to do—I am living proof. The temple I lead is a real child to me, but now it's growing up and even taking an adult name (Panthean Temple). Parental pride swells, and I realize that once I gave myself over to the dream of having a Pagan church, and to Spirit's call, there was no going back. It's a moment on the path that we all face—if you're called, will you answer?

To clarify this process, I'd like to share how the path has unfolded for me personally, in the hope that as you read, you will no longer feel alone or lost. I am a votary of Rhiannon, and she is our temple's matron goddess. It would be impossible for me to tell you this story without including her in it, since she has everything to do with it. Each year at the Feast of Rhiannon, I again tell the tale of my experiences and the series of "coincidences" that have led me here. Without her, our temple would not exist, and I would not be who I am today in body, mind, or spirit.

My introduction to the Old Religion began twenty years ago, when I got some reading materials from a friend, who also escorted me to my first ritual. Still a Christian, I found all this to be very new. Knowing that I was going through a lot of trials, this wonderful woman offered to do a tarot reading for me. She told me a good number of things, but what surprised me the most was what she said about my future. The High Priestess card had come up. She told me that I would be a priestess one day and that I would do something significant for the Pagan community. When I stammered, "But I'm Christian," she replied with a sympathetic smile, "I know, but this is what I see."

About a year later I realized what she already knew—I was a Pagan. Over the next several years, my life and my perspectives noticeably changed—the doorway to the world of Spirit seemed to throw itself open wide. As a child I'd had intense visions, but I really didn't expect them to return. Wrong! It was a vision that changed the direction of my life forever—a goddess came to me and asked if I would serve her again as I had before. She offered me her hand, and I took it without hesitation. I wondered who this Lady was, but the only image that remained in my mind was that of a white horse. When research led me to the name *Rhiannon,* it felt right, but the uncertainty lingered.

I was about to write the vision off completely as imaginary when something else came to my mind unbidden—I was told to go to a store that had just opened up (I had never been there), and that confirmation awaited within. A few days later, I visited the place and discovered white carved bone horse beads on a tray. I bought one and made it into a pendant.

There emerged a list of things that I knew I was supposed to do. It's a kind of a spiritual "honey-do" list from the Goddess, and it seems to grow every now and then (another thing common to leaders, it seems). One of the first items was to form a Pagan church. It made no sense— who was I to start a church? I was supposed to become a priestess as well. That was a pretty tall order, and as a shy, quiet person, I was more than a little intimidated by it.

The discovery of Pagan chat rooms on the Internet was a huge blessing, opening up opportunities for networking and understanding.

From there developed the idea of backyard barbecues for any who wished to find fellowship. Those food-and-fellowship moments allowed us to discuss this crazy idea of a Pagan church, and the idea grew to the point that we named it the Pagan Community Church.

Serendipity seems to have followed the church from the beginning. Shortly after formation, by accident we found a Pagan-at-heart attorney who helped us, pro bono, to incorporate as a church and receive our 501(c)(3) status. Talk about a huge sign from the Divine that this was the right path!

Mind you, having the church set up didn't make things perfect. Learning how to run a Pagan church made me painfully aware of my shortcomings. I had to learn more, and I had to become more. I asked the Goddess for a teacher, and I was pleasantly surprised. My teacher, Rowan, found me in the parking lot of the Department of Motor Vehicles (again, the Divine moves in mysterious and often humorous ways). She turned out to be a priestess from Canada who generously and kindly provided a lot of information and advice that proved invaluable.

Alongside this growth, the Universe requires leaders to change—to shed illusions as a snake sheds its skin. Sometimes even long-term relationships no longer fit the person we are becoming.

At times, things were very uncertain. The emotional and financial drains were not small. When I found myself at the end of my endurance, I turned back to the one stable force—Rhiannon. I told her everything, in detail, with footnotes! True to form, the Lady was not to be undone. The agency that called the next day with a job offer had a front desk adorned with a tall, pale gray horse-head sculpture made of stone, a painting of a white horse inside, and a computer screen saver image of a white Arabian horse.

That job didn't last long, but it led me to other assignments and left enough money for me to focus on both real life and the church. One thing people often forget is that leaders are still people, prone to mistakes and needs and weaknesses. While I was going through some of my personal problems, the church nearly fell apart, and if it hadn't been for a friend, it might never have recovered. Interestingly enough, that friend's home had an unfinished, unframed oil painting of a white horse on the wall, which he had rescued from a trash bin because it had seemed a shame to throw it away. Later he became a housemate and my brother in all but blood, and the church was once again on better footing.

Cycles being what they are, another round of housing difficulties required a break from the church and its challenges. While I was gone, it seemed that much of the "heart" work was neglected. Calls came in from people feeling lost and alone. And again the temptation to just give up crept in.

In trying to find answers, I turned to priests and priestesses I knew and asked them lots of questions about what worked for them and what didn't. I needed to understand why I was constantly reacting to crises and never truly able to accomplish anything in the church as a result. I found my answer, though, from someone in my own church who had been standing on the sidelines and suggested creating more of a layered structure rather than the loose, open one we had: an Outer Court for others to learn and grow within, and an Inner Court for those who do the serious magickal work, which would also refill my spiritual well when it ran dry.

This was profound advice and truly a pivotal point in the church's history. Unfortunately, no one really could guide us on the way to making that turn in the road safely without losing key people from the church, let alone help us handle those who seemed to be abusing it. I decided to visit the Church of Eternal Light, a Pagan spiritualist church. Its pastor, Rev. Marie Langer, and I are friends.

As expected, the idea of Inner and Outer Courts met with resistance, but it was much greater than anticipated. Nonetheless, it was time to take the Fool's leap of faith. I announced the formation of the Inner Court in our newsletter, and quite a lot of people applied—too many. Yet three years later, after our structure changed, the foundation is holding firm. Our members are mature and the church is finally stable. The spiritual work we have been able to do has been an amazing accomplishment, and it shines in the people who are part of it now.

Uniting the community was another of the items on my Goddess's to-do list. Again, this isn't something anyone ever really expects to be called to—let alone accomplish. I came across a powerful message this past year in an email. It read, "The Goddess hasn't brought you all this way to make a fool of you, nor of her plans for you." It's true. And it's true of anyone, anywhere who suddenly realizes this story is their story. The names and faces change, the situations change, but the calling remains firm.

At our recent Beltane (May eve) festival, I watched something very special happen—a dream to which I had given everything I had suddenly came to life. Our theme was "community," and we had achieved it in a completely amazing and transformational way. Our Pagan community came together for the first time as a community in truth. Our differences no longer mattered and seemed to melt away, with friendships taking their place. The love was tangible, as was the magick of the weekend—it was the finest magickal work the members of my temple, and our community, have ever done.

It took a while for it all to sink in, as I realized what we had manifested on all planes. The congratulations and compliments rolled in over email, including quite a number of personal ones for me that really made my day. I can breathe a sigh of relief and relax now that it's over, since it was so much work, but now even my mind can truly rest easy because I know for certain that our temple is becoming what it was meant to be.

Everything happens for a reason; in the end there are no mistakes, and deity moves in mysterious ways. Persistence, determination, and passion will keep you on the path. For me personally, Rhiannon has been my driving force. It's her work that I'm doing.

My story isn't done yet, and every year I will have something new to share at the Feast of Rhiannon. What needs to be done will never be a cakewalk, and there is so much work that lies ahead of me. That list from the Divine somehow keeps getting longer . . . but at least we know we are on the path, and as long as we stay on the path, that's all that really matters.

No matter what happens and how bad it gets, don't give up and don't lose heart. There are bigger and better things that lie ahead if you meet the challenges the gods throw before you. If you are called to serve our community, that is all you need to know. Just answer the call, be true to yourself, stay on the path, and keep doing "the work"—the gods will never abandon you. Always remember you are a part of their plan.

May Rhiannon's hoofbeats echo in your heart.

An Experience Tree

When you have a quiet moment, sit down and think about the odd twists and turns in your life, both good and bad. Make a list of them. From that list begin to assemble an experience tree—a chart that shows where each one of those shifts in the road took you, and how it worked out. If possible, use personally meaningful symbols at each of the crossroads, representing what happened. Slowly, the pattern of your spiritual and mundane life will emerge from the sketch. Celebrate that pattern; honor that pattern. Put it somewhere safe where you can continue the process as new things emerge and old ones fade. This activity acts as a nice adjunct to keeping your spiritual diary.

—Patricia Telesco—

FAMILY RICHES

SIRYN DOLPHINSONG

People may have a large or a small family, or even no family at all. When we are on a path of Paganism, Wicca, Witchcraft, or whatever you call it, it seems natural to start out solitary. Exceptions are people with a hereditary tradition or setting out on a path with a partner of a like mind. There are those who choose to remain alone, but more often than not an itch is felt to find others of the same kind. If you're a Pagan, how do you begin?

I will start off by saying that I'm one of those with a huge family. At least, it is huge compared to the one I grew up with. My Pagan brothers and sisters are sincere, loving, and reliable, and we've been together for a long time. Now, I won't say we haven't had our ups and downs, but this is a dream I've manifested since I was a child. I see most of them at least once every two weeks, speak with them regularly, and think about them often.

You see, at two days old I was adopted by an older couple with no children. I bonded with my Animist father right away. At an early age, I was exposed to all the wonderful things in nature, and we camped every weekend, often traveling the coasts and state forests of Florida. That was until I hit that rebel teen phase, when there was temporary insanity and I thought my parents knew nothing.

We had absolutely no church affiliations, as my father had very little taste for the hypocrisy that often surrounded the mainstream belief systems. I never experienced a lot of social gatherings except when my parents' friends came around for either wrestling and dominoes or a bluegrass session and my father's famous dinners of freshly caught and smoked mullet.

It was very difficult when school forms included questions about ethnicity, as my adoption records were sealed and I didn't know my own heritage. Finally, when I became an adult, I begged my mother for information. Hesitantly she gave me what I needed, and I found my

The sherpa walk

A great friendship activity for a new group is the Trust or Sherpa Walk. This activity works on trust and communication skills and can be done anywhere. The only tools are people and blindfolds.

You begin with a scenario: While flying over a remote part of the world, your plane suddenly loses power and comes spiraling down to Earth. Miraculously, nobody on board is killed in the crash, but as you crawl away from the wreckage, you all look back at the plane just as it explodes in a blinding flash of light. Everyone is blinded. But you must reach help. As you were flying over, you spotted a small mission in the area. If you can only reach it, you'll be okay.

Now, as luck would have it, two local representatives of the Nabu-nobu tribe saw your plane crash and have rushed to the site to help you. The only problem is that members of this tribe don't speak any known language; instead they use a series of clucks, whistles, chirps, claps, and so on, to communicate. Because you are all experts in anthropology, you also know that no one outside of the tribe may touch a tribe member, on penalty of death. The object is to get the blindfolded group from the starting point to the end point safely.

1. Select an area for the Sherpa Walk that is relatively smooth and free from obstacles. The edges of cliffs are definitely not recommended. Be sure that there are no stumps, broken branches, or other impediments that could cause injury.
2. You can set up a few rope barricades for the blind participants to pass under, logs to step over, trees to go around, and so on.

birth lineage. I received the basics from my birth mother, but it was obvious there would not be a relationship. I had one sister, but she was not going to share her mother with anyone. Funny thing was, that family was just as Pagan as my adopted father. They were just more like a raw stone, where my father was like a polished crystal.

When I turned eighteen I moved with a friend to Lewiston, Maine, for a while, drawn I guess to the mysticism surrounding the area. There was Witchcraft, deemed white and black, all around. Old shut-down churches were homesteaded for occult activity, and it was in the papers daily. I met a white Witch who was very kind and told me I had a gift, but not to explore it until I was ready to settle down and be serious.

3. The length of the Sherpa Walk should be about fifty to one hundred meters or longer.
4. Once you reach the site where you have planned the Sherpa Walk, present the group with the scenario.
5. Everyone must put on a blindfold.
6. Select one or two people to be the Nabu-nobu tribe members, and have them take off their blindfolds. Pick people for this role who are likely to play the role well and safely.
7. Have the rest of the group sit down for a moment while you lead the tribe members aside to show them the route and discuss safety. Do this quickly, as the rest of the group is waiting for you.
8. Your Nabu-nobu guides are now ready to guide the blind crash victims to the mission.
9. There is no physical contact allowed between the tribe members and the blindfolded participants.
10. There is no conversation between the tribe members and the blindfolded participants. The tribe members can only make their sounds in order to try to guide.

At the end of the activity, discuss how each participant felt (both the guides and the "crash victims"). How did the activity change your relationship with one another? How did it increase your awareness of communication and your other senses? Add these reflections to your personal magickal diary.

—Siryn Dolphinsong—

In 1990 I was living in St. Augustine, Florida. Everything I encountered seemed to be occult related and brought back many familiar experiences. There were New Age shops opening everywhere. I found a
metaphysical bookstore called Dreamstreet; as soon as I opened its door,
all my stresses seemed to leave my body. I became addicted in a sense to
this feeling, and I visited often, sitting in a hammock reading about Goddess worship and alternatives to the mainstream religions. The smell of
Nag Champa incense filled the air, as did serene acoustical music, and
the merchants spoke in a tone that made you feel welcome and at peace.
I purchased my first *Green Egg* magazine there and my first bumper
sticker, which read, "God is coming back and she is pissed." I used to
buy smudge bundles for cleansing, which helped me on my way to what
would soon be my path. I was still searching, but most groups seemed
very secretive. The older I became the more family was on my mind.

I moved in 1992 to Georgia, where I reside now, and it seemed
right away that rude awakenings were to come on a spiritual plane. No
one had ever asked if I went to church, but now it seemed everyone was
asking, "Where do you attend church?" I felt alienated until I met my
husband, James, who had been brought up a Salvationist until he was
eighteen, when he made the decision that Christianity was not his path.

Together we went to major bookstores, studied continually to define
our path, and purchased an abundance of books related to Witchcraft
and Paganism. Our library grew by leaps and bounds. When the Internet
became available, I started an effort of networking and trying to find as
many resources and locals as possible on a similar path. I followed Wren
and Fritz of the Witches' Voice when they were in Massachusetts and
continued after their move to Florida. Not to be biased, but they have
always seemed to be the most thorough in helping find others and keeping updated on Pagan news. Now they are one of the largest online
resources (www.witchvox.com).

In 1995, my husband and I started our first face-to-face group, and
we met weekly. I was so excited; I finally had the big family I'd yearned
to have. We stayed together and formed a coven. All went smoothly, and
I gained many more friendships by constant online networking.

It seemed my parents were busy traveling and enjoying their retirement, but we regularly kept in touch. Three years went by and I learned

I would lose my father—the one who taught me everything about living and what real spirituality was—to cancer. I left for Florida and took care of him until he passed. My mother stubbornly moved off to be with folks she called family, who, sadly, snubbed me for not being associated by blood.

As time went on, the membership in our coven started to change, mainly because people moved to distant places, but we maintained our strong beliefs and kept our teachings the same. We all learned a lot from one another; we knew we were not experts and that Witchcraft, the way of the "wise," is truly a lifelong path of learning and experiences.

My spiritual family has grown enormously, with close and distant Pagan brothers and sisters who stay in contact. So I have finally fulfilled my biggest dream. My partner and I also travel to places where we can be free with our religious beliefs; we find people who feel the same way we do and assist in educating people on what Witchcraft is all about.

I recommend that anyone starting out on this path begin by studying. I know it can be boring, but some knowledge is better, especially when seeking teachers and friends to study with. Start networking on the Net, or look for books with snail-mail addresses for groups close to your area. Attend festivals and Pagan Pride events, or even place an ad in the paper. This is great when searching for a Pagan family. Or living as a solitary may work for you: I'm sure many who have started out with a large, mundane family just ache to have the peacefulness of solitude.

Manifesting Your Goals

Write down all the things you long for that are feasible to obtain. Ask yourself honestly which are needed and which are wanted. Clip pictures from magazines that represent your goals and hang them on your refrigerator, bathroom mirror, workstation, or someplace you see every day. For instance, if you are dieting, place a photo of someone with a similar (within reason) weight to your goal on your bathroom mirror. This way, every time you look at the image, you are reminded of the goal to be manifested. Each time you achieve a goal, put the picture representing it in a keepsake box. Once all are in the box, start again with new goals if less than a year has passed. On your year anniversary date from when you began, pull all the pictures out of the box and pat yourself on the back for all your accomplishments. This is a great way keep goals on track, and I often start a year this way, doing a manifestation ritual to get things going.

—Siryn Dolphinsong—

WISDOM OF THE WORLD

W ISDOM COMES IN ALL SHAPES AND FORMS, and often from the least expected source. While we would hope to have common sense, most people realize that it's a rare commodity, gained by trial and error. These stories share both the struggle to walk with wisdom as a constant companion and the wonder of its discovery.

CHILDREN'S
PERSPECTIVES

KATELAN V. FOISY

The memorial for my grandmother (*oma* in German) was fast
approaching, and my nephew Hunter had been helping me clean
up the garden for the past few weeks. In one corner of the garden we
had started to build an altar. On it we placed stones, feathers, pictures,
candles, pumpkins, and chrysanthemums. Hunter was having a blast
planting flowers and choosing which stones would go where. At one
point he wiped his brow and asked, "When is the party for the new
oma?" I looked at him, puzzled. "New *oma*?" I asked. "When is the new
oma coming? Everyone said we're having a party for Oma."

It broke my heart. In the weeks we had spent preparing for the
memorial, no one had sat down with Hunter to explain what had happened. He knew that Oma had died, and it was explained to him that
she was watching over us and loving us in spirit. What he gathered from
all the talk of a memorial was that a new grandmother was coming to
take the place of Oma.

As I explained to him what a memorial was, I placed some stones
on the altar while Hunter gathered more objects for it. I was placing

some objects on the ground when I heard Hunter calling my name. I walked over to him. He was crouched down, pointing to something on the dirt driveway. I looked down at what appeared to be a lone butterfly wing. Hunter picked it up, smiled, and said, "Look: it's a butterfly wing. If we put it on the altar it'll come alive. Oma's altar is magickal." I smiled and let him put it in the middle of the altar, not knowing exactly how to explain this one. We went about our day as usual.

The next day Hunter woke up early and ran out to the garden. "Kitty, Kitty, look!" he called. I ran out to see what he was pointing at. When I got to the garden I realized the butterfly wing was gone. It had been windy the night before and the wing had probably blown away. "See," he said. "Oma's like the Earth, she makes things alive again."

I understood then that Hunter understood death in his own beautiful way. He had made sense of it the best he could; and with that I said, "Yeah, she is, isn't she?" A humble reply to the child who also is teacher.

The child within

Do you have children in or around your life? Periodically try to see the world through their eyes. Go outside and make mud pies. Lie belly down in the rich grass and inhale Mother Earth. Turn belly skyward and daydream with the clouds. Release the child within to rediscover the magick that each soul already knows without struggle or uncertainty: the magick of being.

—Patricia Telesco—

AND THE CHILDREN
SHALL LEAD US

PATRICIA TELESCO

One of the most beautiful moments in my spiritual experience took place at a Craftwise festival. I was there with Gavin Bone and Janet Farrar, among other notable speakers, enjoying what could be best called some quality social time (something presenters don't often get). Janet began to share some experiences that had lain heavy on her heart, and the tears began to fall gently on her face. I was dumbfounded and moved by her genuineness, her humanness in the moment, especially with someone who was for all purposes pretty much a stranger to her. Here was someone who had given tremendous amounts of time and effort to our community, revealing the importance of "serving those who serve" to me in a very intimate way. I felt somewhat inadequate to help and at a loss for words.

I went back to my room that night and didn't sleep much. I tried to figure out what I could do . . . then something struck me. Some months previously, a beautiful woman (Cindy from Next Millennium Books) had given me a pink pendant—a stone specifically to help heal the heart and balance emotions. She'd instructed me at the time to pass it along when I found someone else who needed it as much as I had then. But it was *Janet*! I mean, in my mind it was like a fan giving a gift to Cher. You might laugh, but even authors have idols, and I needed to get beyond that feeling. So I tucked my nervousness in a back pocket and offered the pendant to Janet, explaining the significance. Still, I felt as if something in all this was missing. My spirit was restless and out of sorts. Thankfully, the Universe had the perfect fix it.

Later that night, Janet came to me again in tears, but this time tears of joy. Apparently one of the children at the event was ill, and his sister decided that since the kids couldn't participate in the adult rituals, she would organize all the other children to raise energy for this boy's healing. So they did . . . and later his fever broke. Janet's heart was so filled by seeing our next generation step up to being priests and priestesses that her healing began too. She then passed along the stone to the young girl and explained to her mother what it represented. It has now become a marker for our young elders—our future.

This experience taught me many things: the value of trusting your instincts, the need to give energy to our elders and teachers so they don't burn out (even when you're nervous about doing so), and the amazing wisdom our children often bear. A tradition can begin with a simple gesture. Consider starting a meaningful one today.

Learning from our children

There are numerous children in our community. Even if you don't have one of your own, I highly recommend sitting and talking with them about spirituality on more than one occasion. Talk very little—listen a lot. Let them remind you about the wonderful simple things that we often overlook as adults. Most important, don't overlook any chance to empower the future leaders. The young girl in this story gathered a group of youth of many ages, raised energy, and moved proverbial mountains through her determination. If we give each of our children this type of encouragement, we will be creating a future in which leaders have support and novices have a tradition of being able to turn to leaders in trust.

—Patricia Telesco—

GODDESS GIFTS: ALIGNING WITH THE MONETA ENERGIES

SHAE MOYERS RIGHTMIRE, D.DIV.

*Money is divine and money is profane depending
on how we choose to perceive it. Money is an energy,
nothing more, nothing less. I am the one who
chooses to enervate or energize its currency.
Which perception do I choose?*

—Marilyn Lynch—

We as a society have been programmed over centuries to view money as not sacred. We do not give much thought to what money does for us, but focus on what we cannot do when we lack the money energy in our lives. Money is considered dirty, filthy, and unholy. We as human beings are, through the extension of this stereotype, considered unholy or unworthy to be abundant or prosperous because we are limited by our own "lack programming" and centuries of ancestral devaluing of the Moneta energies (named for the Roman goddess of prosperity). How do we return money to the realm of the sacred, to having it as part of our wise ways? It is a challenge; however, it is doable.

At the time the Goddess was at her height, money took the form of barter and trade. Grain was considered the sacred coin because it came from Gaia, the Earth Mother. Legend has it that all forms of commerce were considered sacred acts, and to have plenty was to have been richly blessed by the Goddess. There was no shame in plenty or in having a rich, abundant harvest. Moneta is the money aspect and representational archetype of the financial face of the Mother.

As the Romans created coins and commerce, gold, silver, and copper became the currency of choice. The sacredness of commerce and enterprise became further and further removed from our consciousness as the world's money system became more and more based on power, greed, and a divide-and-conquer mentality. Where once the Mother stood supreme, grain was available to anyone who could harvest it, and a more communal way of living reigned in which prosperity, abundance, and a more equitable sharing of wealth and power were the norm, gradually a patriarchal society with class distinctions, caste systems, and poverty became commonplace.

Money is energy. Money takes on various forms through coin, currency, or an exchange of services and goods. Our challenge today is to return money to the sacred, to view every exchange, purchase, or debt as sacred. We are challenged to rise above age-old stereotypes and internal programming of lack and shame about money. To have too much money is considered gluttony or shameful by our society. To lack enough money is considered martyrdom, laziness, or an unwillingness to receive. No matter how we choose to view our money consciousness, we are surrounded by negative and limiting stereotypes, assumptions, and a fear of not being able to have what we truly desire in our lives. Christianity taught us that it is wrong to have too much money, yet the Bible itself is a book full of prosperity teachings and prophecies of our own sacred birthright to be prosperous and abundant in all ways. We are shown through these teachings the dichotomy of having too much and not enough because of our own limited consciousness and loss of sacred energy around money.

Money is about balance. We balance our checkbooks, we balance our budgets, and we weigh and balance every financial decision we make. In my work, I have found that people who have money issues and who do not view money as sacred have manifested these issues in other areas of their lives. Money is energy that knows no class or racial distinctions. It affects everyone, everywhere in some way. Money issues of every kind simply are the outward manifestation of something within us: the result of old limiting patterns, old programming, and old learned behavior. To deal with shadow surrounding the energy of money is to deal with the darkest parts of our earthly society and ourselves as we know them. It is only by turning within and reclaiming our own birthright of divinity and sacred prosperity that we can begin to return money and its sacredness back to Source.

There is a basic spiritual law that has reigned throughout the ages. It is the principle of *ini,* sacred reciprocity, equitable exchange. The principle of *ini* is simple: it is demonstrated in any exchange in which both parties feel their needs have been met on an equitable level and feel *complete* with the transaction. This principle can be applied anywhere, especially to the energetics of money and any transaction in which this energy is exchanged. The spiritual law of equity and balance in all things is fulfilled in this sacred manner.

We honor ourselves and our earth journey by our willingness to change our thinking. We choose to remember where we come from: from Source. In this remembering, we reconnect with the Moneta energies and remember the sacredness of money in all its forms. Rising from the ashes of past shamefulness and stigmas, we can claim what is rightfully ours as spiritual beings. We reawaken the Goddess within as we consciously choose to walk a more abundant and prosperous life path than that of our ancestors. This is done deliberately, with reverence and without fear or shame.

We must open ourselves to receive, not martyr ourselves or offer ourselves on a monetary level as sacrifices to the powers that be. As we give we must also receive. It is the way of the Universe, the ebb and flow of the energetic money tide in our lives. By cutting ourselves off from Source and disconnecting on a soul level from the universal abundance and prosperity that by birthright is yours and mine, we forget, fall asleep, and slip back to the ways of our old programming.

The old stereotype that you have to be poor to be spiritual is dead. As our society evolves to new levels and people embrace their abundance and prosperity through the discovery of these spiritual teachings, more and more commerce is entering the spiritual realms. The lines between the commercial and spiritual worlds are becoming blurred and fading away as we as a society become more spiritually aware. Practicing this spiritual principle with integrity and embracing our divine prosperity birthright is becoming mainstream. People who choose to make their careers or way of life through a spiritual occupation are no different from those who work in a factory or an office, or who run their own business.

They must practice and stay in harmony with natural law, but also be able to make a living by charging for their services. It is a commonly recognized exchange of goods and services—the same as in mundane commerce. Priestesses and priests of the Goddess face this challenge of walking in balance between these energies on a daily basis. In reality, there is no separation between the two worlds; they are just different views and perspectives of our common humanity. We choose to put up these barriers and separate these worlds because of our own limiting beliefs.

The energy of money is a gift from Spirit. To have it we must be in harmony with natural law and reach out wisely to manifest it in physical form. To deny or cast away this gift is to live out of balance with the law.

So how do we break the cycle? Here are some simple principles to put into practice.

- *Release yourself from the great lie.* Examine your beliefs about money closely and carefully. Often we are not conscious of our beliefs, so they are subconsciously affecting our choices and therefore our lives. Write down every negative belief you have about money, and then beside each one write a new positive belief you now choose to accept as your truth. Deliberately choose what you will believe is possible for you in your life and what your relationship with money and the natural abundance of the Universe will be.

- *Consciously choose to live prosperously.* Decide you will live a prosperous and fulfilling life. Take it as a spiritual practice, because that is what it is. Practice the principle daily. Stay aware of your conviction. Make a pledge of prosperity to replace the subconscious pledge of poverty you may have been binding yourself to.

- *Act accordingly.* Our thoughts and actions create our reality. Align yourself with your good. Instead of buying four pairs of crappy shoes, buy one pair of exquisite ones. Treat yourself like a person of stature, like the successful, happy, and prosperous person you already are.

- *Ask yourself, How must I prepare to receive my good?* If you want clothes, make room in your closet. If you want a new house, buy a pen to sign the mortgage with. Clean out your garage to put the new car in. This is not "what do I need to do to get it?" There is a subtle but very important difference here.

- *Really feel the object of your desire close at hand and prepare to receive it.* If you are replacing an item that is still usable, in good condition, or that someone else would benefit from, offer it as a gift, sell it, or donate it. Don't throw it out! Again, the law of *ini*!

- *Practice generosity of spirit.* Know that you are always provided for. Give especially when you are fearful of not having what you need. When we give freely and generously of what we have, no matter how little or how much, we change our consciousness; we affirm our prosperity to the Universe. Remember, like attracts like.

- *Be grateful for what you have and be open to receive.* Gratitude is one of the most powerful ways that we can align our spirit with the natural abundance of the Universe. Acknowledge the wealth of love, time, intelligence, the blessings you do have, to open the door for more to come in.

- *Make your prosperity and your money energy a journey of awareness.* Truly, when learning the laws of prosperity and manifestation and working with the sacred Moneta energies, we are learning to live in alignment with natural law, balancing our desires with our energy output and healing our sense of separation from Source.

Life is a wonderful journey of liberation and self-discovery when you choose to experience it this way. Abundant blessings and prosperity to you, as you set out on your journey.

COMMITMENT

JESSE WOLF HARDIN

O ur spiritual path resonates with opportunities to understand true commitment. Consider: Magick is deliberately affecting outcomes through the power of our intention and the strength of our dedication. Such commitment is insistence with a direction and a purpose—a promise that, regardless of the degree of difficulty or the result, is each moment honorably met. It's our chance to do the impossible not just once, but again and again, so that the inspirited world can depend on us as we depend on it. It is the gift we give to our beloved, the one we never take back, carefully considered and then pledged first to our real selves and empathic, intuitive, worthy-of-love hearts. What beloved? The land, our families and practices, our causes and clans.

Commitment handfasts us to the object of that commitment, and like a marriage it requires regular attendance and attention. For example, we cannot claim to be committed to a lover unless he or she can depend on us when we're needed. Similarly, one cannot claim devotion to a spiritual practice or path honored only on solstices, Sundays, or Sabbats. The opposite of *committed* is *conditional*—that is to say, being there for loved ones only as long as they retain their money, their novelty, their charm or youthful looks. *Conditional* is honoring and deferring to

Nature and the land only to the degree that doing so doesn't impinge on lifestyle or habit. *Conditional* is sticking with a task or quest only as long as there are clear rewards and results, until it gets difficult, challenging, tedious, or tiresome. In brief, commitment requires completion.

These days we associate commitment with the obligation and rigidity of the money chasers and power brokers of mundane society, but even freedom requires a commitment, to both conscious responsibility and sweet liberty. Nonetheless, spiritually speaking, commitment is the full consignment of the magickal self—with no provision for default, no requirement of success, and no room for regret. One cannot put a price on this devotion, and it's a pledge, deliberately and continuously fulfilled if you're willing to take that challenge to heart and soul.

Commitment is a practice we share in common with the rest of the Universe, and is in fact the fundamental force binding together the swirling, exploding, intercoursing energy and matter of all creation. The sun commits its splendid finite energy, consciously or not—even though it will one day burn itself up in the process—and the very life of this planet depends on that unwavering commitment. The health of plants and animals, fungi and roots hinges on interwoven commitments, together forming the interdependent fabric of the inspirited biosphere. Evolution is a commitment to complexity, relationship, and change. And life itself is a commitment—of Spirit—to its own diverse sentience, manifestation, and expression.

Commitment requires hands-on effort: if we're to dedicate ourselves to truth, we have no choice but to live it and speak it. Similarly, a commitment to the Earth, to the living land—whether to a single section of suburban yard or an entire threatened ecosystem—requires effort, actively doing one's best to protect, tend, restore, celebrate, and resacrament it. Like many seekers, I learned to commit to the Earth, to the ways and the direction of the Holy/Whole, through pledges to a particular sacred place.

For example, there are seven shallow river crossings between where my partner and I park most vehicles and the Sweet Medicine Sanctuary in New Mexico where we live and teach. While we transport gear in our little Jeep, we encourage anyone who can walk to take the time to come in slowly, each barefoot splash of cool river water thrusting us out of our verbose minds and into our creature bodies, alerting us to the real world, awakening not only conscious presence but childlike engagement and delight. Come spring, the roar of new life delivers us into a world of hunger and hope, and the winter is just cold enough to encourage a deep and helpful silence.

When I first arrived here some twenty-five years ago, I thought of myself as a veritable gypsy, loving all places equally and loving the thrill of motion most of all. And if I were going to select somewhere to settle down, I'd already decided it would be the mountains of Montana, or among the beautiful fir and folk near the border between Oregon and California. You can picture my surprise on coming to a halt in the volcanic Gila Mountains of southwestern New Mexico and feeling at home like never before. You can imagine how fortuitous and even destined my arrival felt, as well as how insistent the voices of the canyon were as they whispered and howled and prodded me to stay.

From the moment I came upon this canyon I have been as given to her as to a lifetime soul mate—I was committed! For the first several years I amazed the conservative local ranchers by walking not only the seven river crossings to the road, but the entire ten-mile trip to town for supplies; having sold my truck, my motorcycle, and even the engine out of my converted school bus in order to cover the earnest money necessary to clinch my offer. As you may or may not know, earnest money is a substantial sum of cash deposited with a real estate agent or other third party in order to guarantee you're really earnest about whatever offer you might make. If they reject the offer you get your money back, but if they accept the deal and for some reason you can't come up with the funds you promised, you lose your entire deposit.

Needless to say, I had absolutely no idea how I was going to get the remaining several thousand down. I was relaxing with a book on the Vikings, many years and many annual payments later, when I discovered a historic corollary. It seems there were times when members of a Viking landing party found themselves surprised by a larger and more powerful force. Rather than retreat, on some such occasions, it is said, the chiefs set fire to their ships. With no means of retreat and the sea to their backs there could be no halfhearted swing of the sword, no conditional application of will, cleverness, and might . . . no partial commitment.

Long before this Sweet Medicine Sanctuary had other permanent residents or visiting interns, there was just me: a single soul quieting the mind sufficiently to hear and adhere to the will, the intent, the song of a most special canyon place. Through the turning of the seasons I became increasingly aware of why I was here and what I was meant to do. First I recognized—at the very deepest levels—that the land would mean my personal deliverance and refuge, reassignment and reward. Next it sank in that I was needed here, as much as I needed this place. I was called to give back to the canyon, restoring its riparian forests and indigenous wildlife as well as conserving the archaeological and ceremonial sites here. I knew then that the land was teaching me something—specifically that I had to make it available to all those who needed its unique medicine.

It seems one doesn't seek out or design a life and home so much as answer an ancient, echoing, and ongoing call. At such times it's not only our minds deciding on a saner, more meaningful existence or rationally choosing between interesting groups or places, but rather an irresistible siren song leading us into the moss-draped lap of coastal redwoods or the green bosom of the Rockies, to a farm in the heart of Midwestern grasslands or a certain clan on a particular bend of a destiny-laden river. We are often drawn to a specific bioregion as well as to a new way of being and doing. We're called into intuitive communication and relationship with the larger world, as well as with one another. We learn from the informative land how to best restore, inhabit, and honor it, and how to do the same for our own rewilding selves. It expands and deepens us. It commits us. We're drawn into wordless intimacy through the power of our caring and the seductions of the land, which not only sustains but instructs and affirms us, which reawakens us to the sensuous experience and ageless wisdom of our native selves, which reunites us with the earthen as well as the ethereal. The authenticity, sentience, and joy in the living world become our own as we develop into families and communities both purposeful and placed.

It's only now wholly clear that the entire world is a set of pledges and follow-through, and that the residents of this sanctuary have at a minimum seven primary commitments that link us to self and purpose, Earth and Nature, God/Goddess, and those folks whose hope and home are our own. We're talking not about dogma or rules, but rather a common adherence to and faith in certain basic considerations, values, and goals.

The following are the essential commitments of the Earthen Spirituality Project and Sweet Medicine Women's Center, its permanent residents and long-term students . . . though they certainly not the only commitments. They are also very good commitments for any spiritual soul.

1. *Being.* Right action depends on powerful presence, heightened sensitivity, honest expression, deep connection, and intensity of focus. Our first commitment is to reinhabit fully our authentic, intuitive, feeling selves—fully and consciously in place—in precious relationship and intentional community . . . in vital present time. Be here—right here—now!

2. *Guarding and Celebrating.* We are pledged to protect the ecological and archaeological integrity of the canyon sanctuary and sur-roundings from external threats such as developers and even from our own possessions, preconceptions, and moods. We commit to tuning in to the needs and responses of the inspirited land, rather than simply imposing our ideas, habits, and plans. Much depends on our never compromising the integrity of the land, the inspirited source of our lessons and blessings. This is true of any sacred site. Once you find it, walk gently. Talk little. Listen a lot!

3. *Resacramenting and Restoring.* The sanctuary was not only a large village site but also a primary spiritual center for the Mogollon people living here up until a thousand years ago, and we're pledged to do our best to continue this legacy of conscious ritual tending. The sanctuary land loves being touched, celebrated, and sung to, and to do any less would be negligent on our parts. And as part of a rare Southwestern river ecosystem, it requires contin-uous hands-on reparation, restoring vital wildness and balance after a hundred years of damage and neglect. This includes discerning

what is to be excluded as well as what to reintroduce, and remembering to both celebrate and resacrament this land. If we as a community would celebrate and hold and heal the whole world this way, what wonders we'd create.

4. *Studying.* We are committed to learn—and to learn to apply— the lessons and wisdom offered by this special place. We do this by being truly open, by tuning in to the insights of the canyon and its resident energies, and by manifesting such insights on practical and physical levels. Stay open to the land and the precious lessons it gives you.

5. *Disseminating.* It is our responsibility to make available the spiritual and practical insights given us by this ancient place of power. We need to take the time to record and reach out with the truths that are made so clear here, in this cauldron of inescapable intensity. It is incumbent on us to do everything we can to get the lessons and insights of this land out to those most in need of this message of sentience and activism, of planet and purpose. For us this includes book publishing, writing articles for various periodicals, and positively affecting everyone we meet. What will you share of the sacred lessons Earth teaches? How?

6. *Hosting.* While being careful not to introduce disruptive or dishonorable human energies, we still need to make this portal and shrine available to any earnest spiritual seekers, and to open this home, community, and assignment to the most sensitive, empathic, impassioned, and committed residents. What sanctuaries can you offer to other like-minded souls, even if it's only a moment over coffee?

7. *Extending.* We are dedicated to reestablishing a lineage of protectorship and teaching: training and supporting a community of seekers willing to devote themselves to the sanctuary, the land, its canyon teachings, and the preceding fundamental priorities. Most such seekers will do the essential work from afar, and during periodic stays here. A few will be called and equipped as lifetime inhabitants of this precious inspired place. Theirs is the most substantive burden, the most meaningful commitment, the greatest joy, the most lasting satisfaction. To whom or what will you give your spiritual lineage?

In this age of distraction and destruction we as sensitives are called to do more, to commit to learning and being ever more authentic and aware. Commit to these principles and practices:

- The truth of love and a life of service
- Our spiritual and magickal practice, whatever benign and connective forms that takes
- Actively creating deep, healthy relationships with family, clan, community, and tribe
- Providing the children with the gifts and skills they need to do what seems to be impossible
- Honesty, and contributing to the honest expression of others
- Developing alternative, Pagan, and Earth-centered schools
- Building from the experiences of the elders, and utilizing their wisdom and insight
- Engaging in political dicussion and becoming politically active, or becoming an activist outside the political system
- Planting gardens on rooftops, tearing up concrete and replanting wild seeds, planting wild ideas in those we meet who are too sensitive and wild to "fit in"
- Adopting parks and seeing to their needs
- Demonstrating or legislating for the protection of wilderness endangered by greedy exploitation and soulless development
- Making prayers, incanting, and casting, alone and in groups, directed not toward the superficial satisfaction of our desires, which are our responsibility to meet, but toward the awakening and healing of this planet and its distracted human kind

If I can pass anything on to the students and seekers who make their way here, it's because of what I have learned about commitment from listening to and utilizing the gifts of Spirit, as embodied in Gaia/Nature and communicated through the wondrous river canyon I am given to. I've been shown that hatred and fear may give birth to obsession, but never to commitment. Commitment is an outgrowth of the most persistent love. Commitment is a way of extending ourselves, an investment and a reaching out usually involving some degree of both cost and risk. It is better to fulfill commitments to a few things than to commit to many and fully honor none. In short, we get back gifts of clarity and understanding, discernment and delight equal to the degree we commit our hearts and lives.

Walking back out across the canyon's seven river crossings, we can't help but feel the presence of the ancients who lived here for thousands of years before us. Listen carefully and we can still hear their songs and drums, the laughter of randy elders and boisterous black-haired kids. Look closely enough and behold the absolute interconnectedness and inseparability of even the most shifting of patterns, the designs in cloud and water. Resonating with the vibe of place—and heeding its needs and lessons—gives us most of what we as caretakers, wizards, and priestesses need most for our ongoing mission, our own impeccable being and doing. Our giving back to the land heightens our ability to pass on these Gaian blessings of love, wisdom, and hope to others.

One cannot measure commitment by the poetry of pledges made to entities on wings of wind, nor by timbre of a solemn oath of blood . . . but rather, by the continuity and depth of our presence, the strength of our bond, and doing what we say—and by our heartful, soulful, magickal investment, day after day after day.

Thinking about commitment

- Explore any negative connotations the idea of commitment holds for you. Since no one can force you to commit, you cannot be a victim of even the most difficult or unpleasant commitment.
- Since commitment is your gift, consider carefully in your heart what you might best give it to. To whom? To what? When? How? What will be most meaningful and powerful, let alone transformational?
- Clarify and implement willing commitments to self, lovers or mates, family, friends, allies, clan, tribe, and your fellows of the human species in all their varied and not always agreeable forms—and to the future generations, on whose shoulders may rest the fate of our kind.
- Clarify and implement willing commitments to the greater community of life, the nearest forests and neighborhood creatures: to the personal, hands-on specifics of environmental protection and restoration as well as social change and social justice. To Gaia, the living Earth. And to purposeful Spirit.
- Make all implied agreements with people, places, and causes conscious, explicit, intentional, and verifiable. Be proactive!
- Verbalize and ritualize your commitments in solitude (out in Nature in the presence of roused Spirit), also in circles of witnesses, and when possible among sisters and brethren pledged to the same commitments (and who can help support you in pursuing your goal).
- Nothing is inconsequential. Live fully. Open to the joy of the gladdest burden: caring.
- Decide how you want to be, and how you want to live; then commit to that.
- Until you know where home is, commit to leaving something special every place you go.
- When the time comes, let a place pick you instead of you picking a place. Commit to that home.
- Practice treating every moment as a decisive moment, and no matter what you are or aren't doing, realize that it is your choice.
- Remember that you are given everything you need to meet your promises honorably.
- Regardless of whether you are ready to commit to a lover, idea, or place yet, commit nonetheless to love.
- Be grateful for the commitments of others, the committed nature of Earth and Spirit, and your own capacity to commit.
- Commit always to gratitude.

—Jesse Wolf Hardin—

MINDFULNESS

LADY WILLOW

The dictionary provides the following definitions for the word *mindful:* paying attention, heeding, being cognizant, watchful consciousness, enlightened. One of the first lessons the Goddess taught me as an adult was to recapture the art of mindfulness. As young children, we are naturally aware. Our environment and daily activities are able to teach us because we are open and accepting. As an adult I had forgotten how to pay attention.

When I was a child and teenager, I had always felt a deep need for a spiritual life. I attended many Christian churches and visited with members of the Baha'i faith, but nothing seemed to fit. I was drawn to mythology and all things "occult." I had never heard of Wicca and had no idea that modern-day Pagans existed. I once constructed an altar dedicated to Bast in my bedroom after reading a great deal of Egyptian mythology. I thought I was the only person alive with such an altar.

When I was married, I joined the Christian church of my in-laws' choosing. I tried desperately to be a "good Christian," but after many years I became extremely disillusioned with both the faith and its followers. I knew there was a path for me, but I didn't know where to look. I scanned the religion section of the newspaper and visited various churches. Finally I did what I should have done all along: I spent an evening in quiet meditation and asked any deity who would listen to send me direction. But most important, I promised to listen—to be mindful—and I did just that.

Over the course of the next couple of years, some amazing things began to happen. I received a catalog in the mail advertising Celtic harp music and ordered a CD. I had never listened to that type of music before. It took me to places I can't begin to explain. I began to have dreams of people worshipping around a bonfire. Books by Starhawk and Margot Adler literally fell off the shelf in front of me at the library. I received in the mail an unsolicited copy of Circle Sanctuary's newsletter. Copies of the "Old Law of Knowledge" began showing up everywhere: tacked on a neighbor's refrigerator, on a videotape I rented, and so on. The list of signs and messages is long. But the point is that I became mindful or aware of the information being sent to me.

All this led me to Celtic Wicca, which not only felt like my spiritual home, but took me back to my ancestral roots as well. Although it has been twelve years since this process began, I continue to be reminded of it whenever I find myself becoming too busy and out of touch. We need to remember to be mindful, to be receptive to whatever lessons are ours to learn.

cultivating mindfulness

This is an exercise I learned during the period of my life that I have described. It opens the mind and the heart, creating the mindful disposition. It's a Cherokee tree ritual (a similar ritual is found among other Native American tribes). This version is adapted from *Living Deliberately,* by John H. McMurphy, Ph.D.

Go to a quiet place in nature where you will not be disturbed. There must be at least one tree, preferably several. Choose a tree that "calls out" to you. You will be asking the tree four questions correlating to the four cardinal directions. Before asking each question, lovingly place an offering of cornmeal and tobacco at the base of the tree. Stand with your back against the tree and become one with the tree and with the moment. Lie under the tree facing south and ask the tree, "Who am I ?" Wait patiently for a response. Your response may be an inner impression or image, an external image or symbol (a vision), an inner voice or intuition, or an external, audible voice. Be patient and let the tree answer in its own manner. Be open to whatever insight you receive.

Repeat the process, asking the following questions while facing the following directions. Face north and ask, "What is my purpose?" Face west and ask, "Where did I come from?" Face east and ask, "Where am I going?" After each question, wait again patiently for a repsonse.

Go to the direction in which you received the answer that felt the most powerful or stimulating. Place your forehead against the tree. Give to the tree anything (a problem, a limiting thought, a fear) you wish to let go of at this time. Thank the tree for sharing its wisdom with you and for accepting what you have left with it. Hug the tree and offer it more cornmeal and tobacco. You may wish to stand back from the tree and spend a few minutes in humble appreciation for what the tree means both to you and to nature.

—Lady Willow—

SWEET DREAMS: A JOURNEY TO RESTFUL SLEEP AND THE WISDOM OF DREAMING

GAIL WOOD

"Sweet dreams," my mother would say as she tucked me into bed during my childhood. "Sweet dreams," she would call when I trudged my teenage self to my room. "Sweet dreams," she would say as she went to bed and I stayed up to all hours during my college years. Never a demonstrative woman, my mother has always made those two words into a bedtime hug and kiss.

"Sweet dreams," I said to my partner, Mouse, the first night we spent together. He held me close and told me that no one had ever given him such a loving wish before. To me, those two words are the symbol of everyday love, the sweet affection and warmth of intimacy, the love and wisdom that develop between people who know each other's faults and strengths.

And yet, my sleep and my dreams haven't always been sweet.
I would toss and turn, fretting about the day's events. My nights would
be disturbed as I awakened to worry about the next day, the next week,
or the next month. No situation was too small to escape the attention
of my worrying. From the state of my finances to dirty looks and harsh
words from a coworker, I mulled over every small mistake I made and
agonized over all decisions, great and small. Because my nights were
fraught with worry and sleep disruptions, my days were wearied and
anxious.

A dozen years ago, a friend told me that I deserved a good night's
sleep and recommended seeking some help from either a therapist or a
confidant. It was a new idea, a revelation that sleep could be a peaceful
rest and that I deserved it in my life. I had never imagined any other
way to spend the night, since my own mother had similar sleep patterns.
This new idea of a good night's sleep enchanted me; I decided to approach
it magickally, so I sought help from the Goddess.

I realized that the first thing I needed to do was to get to sleep.
I needed to control the worrying that kept me tossing and turning,
restless and wakeful. Intellectually, I knew that incessant fretting about
everything was a waste of time and I needed to occupy my mind with
other thoughts. I began to collect affirmations that would help release
my mind from this useless cycle of distracted worry. A popular quote on
a needlework design said, "I know that worry works: 90 percent of what
I worry about never happens!" I extended the wisdom in that statement
and transformed it into "Why worry? Ninety percent of what I worry
about never happens."

I then got a bumper sticker that said "Magic happens" as an affirmation that good things happen to those who expect it. When I began to
be trapped in the endless mental cycle of what-ifs, I would remind
myself that magick happens and firmly push those negative thoughts away.
I began to make lists when things were bothering me. If it was a needless worry, I would cross it off the list and push the negative thought
away. If it was something that needed handling, I would either take care
of it or set the thought aside for the appropriate time. It took some discipline to train my thoughts into more positive ways of belief.

One of the important things I did was develop a meditation that guided me to sleep. I chose my absolute favorite place in the world and developed a meditation that led me there. I focused the meditation on the details of the journey, with all the sights, sounds, and smells associated with that place as well as the feelings that I experienced along the way. My favorite place is the beach at the Assateague Island National Seashore, on one of the barrier islands off the coast of Maryland. The meditation focused on driving into the parking lot and going down to the beach for a swim. I made it a rule that if an extraneous thought entered into my mind, I would to go back to the beginning and start over again. It worked, and after a few weeks of this practice I was usually asleep before I made it to the shoreline.

The meditation is below, though the written version is not as detailed or vivid as in my own mind, because my imagination fills in many more visual and auditory details. I encourage you to develop your own meditation based on the things that hold the deepest meanings for you, so that it speaks to your heart and soul.

I drive the car into the parking lot and note that there is horse poop around from the ponies that live on Assateague. I park the car near the bathhouse and get out. I feel the heat of the macadam and feel the sunlight shining its bright light. I shut the car door and lock it with a beep. I walk to the sidewalk and walk between the women's bathhouse and the changing shelter. I hear the water dripping inside the bathroom. I come to the edge of the bathhouse and see the outdoor showers along its wall.

I turn on the shower and rinse off my feet. The water is very cold. I continue my walk, and the sidewalk changes to boardwalk. The little valley of sand below the dune has picnic tables and grills. No one is there. I stand for a minute below the dunes and hear the sound of the waves in the distance, the cry of the gulls. I breathe deeply and smell the salty air and the beach grasses. I begin the walk uphill on the boardwalk toward the crest of the dunes. I notice the individual boards of the walkway as I move up the rise. My anticipation rises as I near the top of the dune. I hear the sounds of the waves, and the wind becomes brisk.

I take a deep, excited breath as I reach the crest of the dune and get my first glimpse of the ocean. Looking out into the far distance, I see the horizon and the ocean that goes on for miles. I hope to see dolphins because I have more than once. Moving my gaze to the shoreline, I see the flags around the lifeguard station. People are jumping along the shoreline and swimming out in the water. As I take a deep breath of wet, salty air, I breathe in ecstasy. I breathe deeply and happily as I walk down into the sand, crossing the beach to the water.

My feet sink into hot, fine sand as I begin my walk. My hips swivel as I sink deeply and then lift my feet. I walk toward the waterline, passing people sunning themselves. Under umbrellas, on blankets with radios blaring, people are enjoying the beach. Kids are playing in the sand, and the lifeguard's ATV sits next to the lifeguard station. Floats and other paraphernalia surround me on the sand. I can smell the suntan lotion that is slathered all over the beached bodies, that sweet coconut scent.

I turn my attention to the shoreline. The sand is wetter now at the high tide line. My feet feel the squish of damp sand. As I get closer, I see three sandpipers running and then poking their bills into the wet sand. They move swiftly onward, seeking food. The sand is very wet, and a wave hits the shore and creeps toward my feet.

Joyfully, I move swiftly to greet the water. Another wave breaks around my ankles, and the spray splatters me up to my thighs. It's cold! I move into the water a little bit at a time. The waves call to me, and my body answers their rhythm. Up to my hips, the water is cold at first and then warms me. Up to my waist, I gasp as a wave surprises me and I get wet up to my neck.

I take a deep breath and a lot of courage and jump headfirst into the next wave. The exhilarating movement and cold move over me, around me, and through me as I rush into joy. I break the surface and look around for the next wave. Up and over. Up and over. The tang of salt is on my lips and in my mouth. The smell of the salt water fills my being, and I joyfully move in unison with the water.

Out beyond the breakers now, I lie back and float. I merge
with the water and the Ancient Mother holds me and rocks me.
Gently up and over. Up and over. The waves carry me. I merge
with the Universe and merge my thoughts with the realm of sleep
and dreams. Blessed Be.

As this meditation began to work its magick, I turned my attention to
my surroundings, transforming my sleeping space into sacred space. I
started with everyday details, such as ensuring that I was surrounded by
colors and things that evoked pleasant feelings and memories. I removed
things associated with work and brought in things associated with relaxation. So my papers and reports from work stayed on the table in the
living room, and I brought in books for pleasure. It was at that time I
began the habit of making sure that my clothes from the day gone by
were either hung up or put into the laundry hamper. This turned out to
be a powerful act. Later, I realized that I was putting away the worries
of the day, either to be dealt with at the appropriate time or to be
washed away completely. Instead of being just another room to pick up,
work in, or clean, my bedroom became a haven and a retreat for deep
and healing sleep.

I bought a statue of the Dreaming Goddess of Malta, an ample goddess lying on her side in an ornamented dress and cradled in what looks
like a dish. Her generous body is in a state of complete relaxation, already
in tranquil sleep. I placed her dreaming there beside my bed. Each night
I would touch my hands to her hips and breathe deeply. With an exhaled
breath, I let go of worry, and with an inhaled breath, I breathed in serenity.
I let go of dissatisfaction and breathed in stillness. Then I would whisper
a short, simple prayer. It was never scripted, just a simple plea to relieve
my stress and bless my sleep.

I also decided to make a pillowcase as a charm for sleep. I chose a
fabric that meant something special to me, with stars and a dark background representing my joy in the dark as well as the light. I called on
my matron goddess—Ariadne, the spinner of thread—to bless my work
as I sewed. I called in animals to accompany me on journeys: the polar
bear to bring me the power of hibernation and the wolf to bring me the
power of safety. They watched over me as I sewed this simple pattern

and let its energy carry over into my sleep. The pillowcase was done and became another addition to my refuge for deep sleep.

Over the years, I have developed into a very sound sleeper. Rest and relaxation are mine as I claim the sleep that I deserve. With the help of the Goddess and the powers that accompany me on my daily journeys, I was able to break an inherited pattern and create another that is magickal and blessed. I've also made the pillowcases as gifts, including with them a dream journal and this poem.

And in the Dark

The sun sets and your head is pillowed by clouds.
Starlight and moonlight dim
Before the power of your dream.
And in the Dark, the soul sings and the heart listens.
In the Dark, the dream gives voice to the Goddess.

In her crescent light, she sings and she spins
The gossamer thread of the dream.
In her full light, she sings and she weaves
The magickal pattern of the dream
And in the Dark, she cuts the cloth and ties the thread.
In the Dark, the dream gives form to the God.

In the springtime, he dances adventure into the dream
And in the summer he dances wildness into the dream.
In the fall he dances bounty into the dream
And in the Dark, he dances death into the dream.
In the Dark, the dream gives life to you.

Paradoxically, in finding refreshing and sound sleep, I became unable to remember my dreams. I felt that it was an excellent trade-off, since most of my dreams had been full of anxiety and stress. Whatever lessons I needed to learn didn't have to be given to me during sleep. I could learn them in my waking life or at a level so deeply unconscious that they didn't need to visit me during sleep. I had become somewhat selfish about my deep, good night of sleep. In a way, I was accepting half the gift and denying myself the other half of the blessing—the wisdom of dreams.

The Goddess would not let me have a life half lived, so she presented me with a lesson on dreams. Dreams, I learned, are messages, bits of wisdom, and lessons from the Divine, and they are a vital part of our lives as Witches. In denying myself a dreaming life, I was denying the Goddess an opportunity to talk to me. I was also denying myself a chance for wisdom and growth. I had to struggle with that realization for a while because I was fearful of returning to the old sleep patterns and anxiety-saturated dreams.

I turned again to the Dreaming Goddess of Malta. My prayer was a simple chant, acknowledging my struggle and asking for a chance to dream.

> To sleep I surrender
> For dreams I remember.
> My dreams are a treasure
> Of wisdom and pleasure.

I made a special pillowcase for this new journey into the realm of sweet dreams. I chose a fabric that signifies my affinity for the dark moon. I called on Ariadne as the spinner of dreams and the mistress of the labyrinth to take me into the deep mystery of dreams. I asked the owl to give me the wisdom of discernment, to enable me to tell the difference between the messages of wisdom and the anxieties of daily life. I asked the polar bear to bring me a sense of adventure and joy when diving deep into the dark waters of the subconscious and the consciousness of the Universe.

Sometimes I remember dreams and sometimes I don't, but I have faith that I will remember the wisdom conveyed in them. Often I get snippets of poetry and meditations to write down. Insights into my daily dilemmas sometimes come to me in my dreams; or I will wake up with a song in my head, and it's not usually something I've heard the day before. Somewhere in the lyrics or the rhythm I find some kind of nugget of wisdom. It's like a postcard from the realm of my subconscious, or from that vast magickal territory inhabited by wonder and love. "Sweet dreams," I call to myself as I am carried off to sleep, safe in the arms of the Goddess.

A sweet Dreams pillowcase

Here are simple instructions for creating your own dream pillowcase. For one standard-sized pillowcase, you'll need

1 yard of fabric, cotton or cotton-blend, washable and soft in texture
Thread
Sewing machine, iron, scissors, pins, ruler, and other sewing supplies

Cut the fabric into two pieces along the width of the fabric, from selvage edge to selvage edge. Piece A should be 12 inches long and piece B should be 24 inches long.

Stay-stitch all raw edges.

At one end of piece A, press one-fourth of the piece in toward the wrong side. Stitch.

With right sides together, the raw edge of piece A to the one of the ends of Piece B, stitch a 5/8-inch seam. Press the seam open.

With right sides together, match the selvage edges, pin, and sew a 5/8-inch seam, matching the seam that joins A and B together. Press the seam open.

At open end of piece B, with right sides together, sew a 5/8-inch seam. Press the seam open. Where the two seams meet, trim the juncture to 5/8-inch seam.

At the end of piece A with the 5/8-inch turning, press up an additional 3/8-inch, press, and sew as a hem.

Turn the whole thing right side out. It is finished. Sweet dreams and blessings, bright and dark.

—Gail Wood—

DISCOVERY
THROUGH DREAMING

ANN MOURA

I was raised in a family tradition of the Craft passed to me by my
Brazilian mother as she learned it from her mother. My grandmother's
maternal line included Gypsy heritage from Andalusia and Iberian Celtic
heritage from Galicia. Growing up for me included magick, spirit communication, and divination as a normal part of everyday life, and it was
not until later school years that I realized things were different for my
peers. My mother was adept at dream interpretation, so asking about
dreams and discussing their meanings were part of our daily morning
conversation—but only after we had something to eat. This was her way
of ensuring we were grounded (as with eating or drinking something
after a ritual, meditation, or magickal working) and preventing the
dream state from entering into the awakened state of the physical world.

From these talks, I gained an understanding of my dreams and an
ability to aid others with interpreting their own. My mother always
emphasized trusting personal intuitive feelings relating to a dream, but
she tempered that trust with the knowledge that some dreams were
"dreams of contrary," wherein the message is the opposite of what is

experienced in the dream state. Anger or shouting often portends some good news, for example, and weddings may portend funerals, while funerals may portend births or weddings. My mother and I would talk through our dreams together to explore their meanings and wisdom.

Later in life I started keeping dream journals, and I have found them to be a valuable tool for tracking the types of dreams I have and then comparing my initial impressions to events that actually transpire. With the passage of time there have been some dreams whose impressions were so strong, vivid, and meaningful on multiple levels that I have never forgotten them. You may wish to begin a dream journal if you haven't already.

Dreams offer an avenue for predictions and divinations, but also for personal enlightenment and discovery. By asking a question or putting a problem out to the Universe before going to sleep, you can trigger a response that will show you answers and elevate your awareness, sometimes even bringing you into contact with deity images you may have not thought about in the past. When this happens, you are expanding your horizons, embracing wider aspects of the Divine and connecting with the ancestors. I fully believe that we travel from one life to another, passing through different cultures and races, changing sex, and exploring a variety of social roles, all to add to our knowledge and our experience of incarnate life. Sometimes we have a single-minded purpose, other times we are simply dabbling to see what one kind of existence or another would be like. I like best the Hindu description of life as play, or *lila*.

When I was a teenager seeking my life path, I had a dream that included my spirit guide. My guide is a very bright light who has traveled with me as I reincarnated through several lifetimes after a time we spent together. I had already felt a desire to be a teacher in this life, but I knew there was something besides history that I was supposed to teach. Because of my trust in my guide, I dreamed an amazing double-cycle dream—a repeated dream cycle in which you pass through a dream and then immediately dream it again, perhaps making changes.

Psychologists encourage people with nightmares to go deliberately back into a dream and change it so the fear is dispelled by taking control of the outcome. But the dream I had was not a nightmare—it was an experience. What I experienced is also known as a shamanic death, which is accomplished in Native American and Aboriginal traditions through training, fasting, and solitary meditation for the purpose of gaining a guide and ease in communicating with spirits and working within the spirit realm. I already had a guide and knew who he was and how we were connected, so while my mind had been on my spiritual path, I was not following such a discipline. The experience simply came, I believe, because I was honestly seeking my path.

In my dream, I was dressed in a long white robe with loose sleeves, standing alone on an open, desertlike plain. I spotted a huge lion racing toward me snarling and growling, and so real was this dream that I was paralyzed with terror. He attacked me at once, knocking me down, and I knew my weak struggles were useless against this immensely strong animal. With a distraught sense of my own doom, I felt the beast close his powerful jaws around my head. I heard and felt my bones crunch in his jaws, and I *knew* that I was dead. At that instant, something I'd learned from psychology passed through my awareness: that dying in dreams never actually happens because people wake up just before the instant of death. Yet I felt on a deep, soul-wrenching level that my death in the dream state coincided with my death in the physical world.

At this point my guide appeared, took me by the hand, lifted me to my feet, and vanished. The lion was also gone, and I stood as before, alone on the dry, hot plain. Suddenly the great beast was racing up to me again, only this time I felt serene and unafraid—was I not already dead? The lion stopped in front of me, roaring and showing the sharp fangs in his terrible jaws, but now I put forward both my hands and gently closed his mouth. With the lion standing calmly at my side, my guide reappeared, nodded, and smiled at me, and I awoke.

Since I am a Leo by birth sign, the dream imagery was especially powerful to me. In retrospect the next morning, I understood that my guide had kept watch over my physical body while I went through the death in the jaws of the lion. I also knew that as many of the showman-ship characteristics associated with my zodiac sign do not manifest in me, so on another level I was holding shut the more vocal and flamboyant aspects typical of the Leo personality.

At the time I had the dream, I was unfamiliar with the tarot deck. Tarot cards were in those days not readily available in America. A few years after the dream, I was drawn to the Rider-Waite tarot deck in a store and bought it. I was quite surprised and delighted by the depiction of the Strength card in the Major Arcana, for it showed a woman in a white gown holding shut the mouth of a lion—the very image of my experience. So on yet another level, I was pathworking with an archetype card I did not know existed, encountering what presaged the action being enacted on the card.

On still a different level, the dream told me that I would hold back for a time on expressing my heritage, for it took several decades and the passing of my mother before my teaching path moved into writing books, giving talks, and conducting classes on the practice of Green Witchcraft. But always the communication with the spirit realm has given me comfort and aid when needed. As it did with me, a powerful dream can return to your awareness repeatedly, helping you tap into the hidden nuances of its meaning throughout your life.

While some dreams occur spontaneously, you can also prime the dream state to answer specific questions or address a problem. I believe that every dream we have is stored in our memories, and when an event takes place later on that relates to the message in the dream—even if several years or even decades have passed—we are suddenly able to understand a new level of significance of even the most arcane dream. Instead of eliciting a sensation of disappointment that you didn't comprehend the significance of a dream from the outset, this type of recall is like an awakening, and you know that a profound discovery has occurred.

This is what happened to me when I had a dream when I was a child of twelve that remained etched in my memory until I discovered its meaning several years later. The impact was a powerful revelation for me that has continued to fill my life with both joy and peace.

The background to the dream came from being invited by a friend to attend her church in summer so she could get points in an outreach contest. We spent the summer going to the meetings and participating in a number of enjoyable social events, all tempered with religious instruction. In one sermon, we were told that God will grant our prayers, but in the same sermon we were told that no one could see God since doing so would destroy a person. We were all reminded to pray at night and ask God for whatever we needed. To me this was a contradiction that begged for exploration, so I prayed for God to show himself to me without causing me harm.

That night I had a wondrous dream. I was walking to the church with my friend, and many people from the congregation were standing outside along with the preacher, who was greeting people by the open front doors. A loud and melodious sound exploded overhead, and everyone looked up. I saw two large shapes arc across the sky, crossing paths to stop in midair above the church, with one to the left and the other to the right of my view. The shape on the left was a huge gold ring, while the shape on the right was a matching gold ring only with golden tongues of flame evenly spaced around it. The congregation was exclaiming, "It's the Second Coming!" in excited anticipation, which diminished as disappointment grew and people milled around, muttering, "Why aren't we rising?" Eventually they shrugged the matter off and went inside the church with their pastor, while I remained outside. Then I awoke.

A few years later, while flipping pages in a history book, I understood my dream. There was a photo of a statue of Shiva dancing in a circle of flames that looked exactly like the one in my dream. God had answered, and he was Shiva. I felt at once that the other gold ring symbolized the moon, and thus I was reminded that the God and the Goddess are the Divine. Now, at this time my mother used a slender, graceful Thai statue of a seated deity to represent the God at home; she burned incense in front of the image daily but never referred to the image by any name. She and her mother both called on various saints for magickal works as aspects of the Divine, but I knew from childhood that Bendis was the name of our secret family goddess. She is the Thracian goddess of the dark moon and of Witches, holding in her hand a twig that points the way to the Underworld. My mother would not

name the god, however. She would get very furtive and aloof, saying
only that he is good. Then I learned that *Shiva* means "beneficent". Was
she translating the name for me? Did she fear I might mention the name
to my playmates as I had unthinkingly done in my childhood with Bendis?

I do not have the answer, but the night she passed, my mother asked
to see what I carried in a pouch on a strap around my neck. I told her it
contained a little man, and when she insisted on seeing, I showed her
my little statue of Shiva sitting in a yogic position on a mound with his
trident upright in the ground behind him, his drum that beats out the
life of the Universe resting beneath the three tines. She said with delight,
"Oh, that is Shiva! I gave one just like that to my brother when he went
to medical school." She confirmed that the god who responded to my
question through my dream was indeed our family god, and since I had
already learned this for myself, there had been no reason to tell me.

It was this particular episode that made me realize there must have
been many things that had gone unspoken in my family simply because
the Craft was approached as so much a part of our routine life, with
nothing about it considered out of the ordinary, so that even burning
incense in front of the image of an unnamed god hardly created a ripple.
It was this incident that prompted me to start putting our oral heritage
in writing for future generations to embrace and adapt as they desired.
The dream that identified God for me is as clear today as when I first
dreamed it more than forty years ago—a potent reminder that dreams
are powerful tools for instruction, guidance, wisdom, and inspiration.

A Dream Notebook

Before going to sleep, ask the God and the Goddess for something you want
to know, a solution to a problem, another perspective on a situation, or any
other matter on which you desire guidance. Then write down your dreams in
a notebook for the next two weeks and see what you learn. Sometimes the
answer comes right away, but other times it may take a couple of weeks for
you to release the request in your dream state so that it can be answered.

—Ann Moura—

TEARS

BEV RICHARDSON

In the late winter and early spring of 1991, my partner, Del, and I decided to settle: buy a cheap property and rebuild it ourselves. A familiar enough dream. We had been twenty-five years on the road, fifteen of them entirely horse-drawn. And now, with half our family grown and ourselves coming into young middle age, we felt a need to find a bit of comfort away from the pressures of roadside living. The house came in the form of a cottage on an acre in the north of County Cork, near the small town of Buttevant.

By dint of some family intervention and selling of horses and wagons, we raised the cash and took possession of the house on April 1, 1991. All that spring and summer, we gutted and rebuilt the house with help from our family, who were all camped in the area. Approaching the end of October, the house, although unfinished, was just about ready for a housewarming party, which we were hoping to hold sometime in early November.

And then, on a wet Thursday afternoon about four o'clock, everything changed. As a family we began a very steep and painful learning curve. Two very pleasant young policemen came to tell us that Aimi Becket, our eldest daughter, had been involved in a traffic accident and was in the local hospital. It was "very serious." I felt as though a hollow pit had opened in my stomach, and I couldn't accept that this beloved girl, so full of life, could be anything but slightly hurt.

When we contacted the hospital, we were told that she had brain damage and had been moved to the main city hospital's neurological unit. This, I feel, is where my individual, personal part in the story begins. The next-door farmer sent his son to take me to the hospital in their car. I suppose I arrived there about half past six or seven o'clock at night, at which time Becket was out of the neurological unit and being put in a bed all wired up to the life-support machines. That is how I first saw her, lying on her back with tubes coming out of her nose. The only parts of her that were working were the breathing and the heartbeat.

Through the night, my son Thomas and other members of the family came and stayed with me and her, along with her boyfriend, John, who'd seen the accident. We sat in a little room beside the ward, trying to talk about anything but what was happening. By ten o'clock Friday morning, I had seen the doctor in charge, who told me what the healer in me had already seen—that my beautiful girl was an animated husk lying in the bed. Her strong farrier's hands warm to the touch, her skin slightly flushed, her heart beating, a breathing empty doll. At this stage the tears were all bottled up inside, and my pain was quite terrible. Still, they told me they had a couple more tests to make, tests that they would then repeat again, twice, just to make absolutely sure.

The unctuous attentions of the Roman Catholic chaplain were not very helpful. In the end I just had to tell him to go away. The result of this was that half an hour later I had to deal with the sad, ineffectual man who was his Protestant counterpart. He at least had the good grace not to offer hope, and to go away without apologizing for his intrusion.

All through Friday, and that evening, the hardest thing to bear was the cheerful optimism of family members. Second-eldest daughter Faie was back from Wexford that night and came with Del to see her. I could see and feel in Del's eyes and heart that she'd just come to say farewell; it was obvious to both of us that what lay on the bed no longer housed the brightness that had been our beloved girl. The hospital had kindly provided me with a little room with a bed in it, though that Friday night

I didn't use it. I just walked around, intermittently going in to sit with Becket. Still no tears.

On Saturday morning, the young doctor came to tell me that the final tests were to be done that afternoon, but frankly there was absolutely no hope. As far as they could possibly tell, her brain stem was severed, though apart from some bruising on the arm and on the side of her head, there was no apparent damage to her strong, healthy body. I think it was at this point the realization came to me that I now had to deal actively with this situation . . . and it was just as though I heard her voice. She had discarded this body, and there was much of it that would benefit others.

So in honor of her desire, I set in motion an interview with the young doctor in the hospital who dealt with transplant requests. She was very helpful and explained to me what their best-case scenario was in regards salvaging organs. By three o'clock Saturday afternoon I had all the papers arranged and signed, and a few small conditions of my own agreed to.

I suppose it must have been about seven-thirty in the evening when I left my son Thomas and John keeping watch and went up to lie down in the little room. There I somehow fell into a deep and dreamless sleep, to be woken up, I suppose sometime around ten, to hear that they were wheeling her into the operating theater. So I went down and walked alongside the trolley, holding her hand. At the theater, she went one way and I was left behind at the door. At this stage, the young men, totally exhausted, were offered a lift back home, so I was now alone with my ghosts.

I went back to the little room and fell asleep again, to be awakened about three hours later by one of the hospital porters, with Ian and Lise, two very dear friends, and as near as Becket ever got to having godparents. They had traveled from Scotland, down through the north, hardly stopping till they arrived to support me, and I could not have had two better people beside me. By the time I got up, washed, and composed myself, the same porter came back to tell me that it was time . . . time to fulfill the last of my conditions and the last thing in this physical world that I could do for my beloved girl.

I know that at this stage, switching off the life-support machine was no more than a symbolic gesture; nevertheless I felt that I could not allow a stranger to do it. This deeply intimate moment was entirely a family affair. In my memory's eye I can remember every step through those quiet, half-lit, past-midnight hospital corridors. It was like some processional as, with Ian and Lise at my shoulders, the hospital porter held all the doors open for us. We finally came to the operating theater. The machines hummed, and her cheek had taken a cooling waxy pallor as physical death settled over her. The Indian doctor in attendance bowed to me and took my hand and put it on the plug, saying, "This is the one," and then stood back.

I had tied that afternoon a quoit of grass, a Gypsy pattern, a family way-mark. Kissing her hand, I closed it over this. In my mind's eye, I took the halter off a bright young filly and, pulling the plug, wished her a good journey. Then, kissing her on the lips, I turned my back forever on the last mortal remains of my firstborn.

As I left the theater, a beautiful young woman in a green gown, one of the young surgeons, stopped me with tears in her eyes and said to me, "It's so hard, we cannot for our own sake take all of this on board, but I know this one is special and I won't forget it. What am I to do?" All I could think to say was, "Just be beautiful; that's all you need."

For the drive home I was glad to have Ian and Lise with me. As we pulled out of the hospital grounds, the helicopter buzzed overhead, heading to Dublin with Becket's gift of life to others. At home, in the three-quarters-finished house, I could only hold Del close and feel the tears bubbling up inside of me—still unsheddable.

The next days were so very busy, moving horses around, arranging funerary doings. Her body was taken to Dublin to be cremated, and Francis Finn—a very dear friend to the traveling people—took it upon herself to return the ashes the following Saturday to the roadside near Killavullen where Becket had made her last camp.

That morning Del and Faie had gone down and scrubbed her wagon out, laying out all her belongings and treasures. All through that midday and early afternoon, her friends and extended family gathered from near and far. Many took away a final gift from among her treasures and left behind a treasure of their own. One old friend even returned a tool he'd borrowed years before.

Then, as the sun started to slant low, with all the tribe gathered and with the help of a good brother, I put a fire to the wagon. I remember feeling very calm and walking into the wagon as it started to blaze, and just sitting there a couple of minutes, thinking how easy it would be just to stay there . . . then her voice came yet again: "Don't be a fool; walk away."

I walked out as the flames were starting to roar. I threw my hat back into the fire. It had a silver horse cutout of an old Irish half-crown coin that she always admired. Then the tears hit home. I could feel the whooping sobs rising, joining the roaring flames. As we stood around the great fire, watching it collapse to a pile of glowing ashes, I don't know how it happened, but somehow I felt myself wading through the burning ash on my hands and knees. I was wearing leather and wool, and wasn't too badly burned. Guess it shocked me back into some kind of sensibility, the poet's eulogy ringing in my head.

Then back for the wake, which was a strange mixture of feelings, and true to traveler custom didn't manage to pass over without a couple of fights. By this time, however, I was too drunk and cried out and exhausted to notice. The next four years were spent in a painfully distressing uphill battle with the Irish legal system, which taught me truly the meaning of "fallen amongst thieves." After four years of painful reiteration, at the last possible moment the insurance company settled. By this time, of course, the lawyers had profited as much by it as our grandsons. So there you have it.

For the gift of tears, my eternal thanks.

For the gift of her too-short life, my thanks.

One year to the day at the ash pile that was the remains of her wagon, I stooped to the burned ground and without looking picked up the blackened cutout horse coin, returned through fire. Our granddaughter now has it polished as her birth piece from Becket. The main lesson I had from all this is that we are a spirituality of mutual love and care; our strengths come from the living love of the planetary being that nurtures us to be fully human . . . to be fully aware, fully wise, fully alive even when the wheel of life turns yet again.

NATURE'S ADVISERS

A s "PEOPLE OF THE EARTH," Neopagans have a special place in our hearts for Nature and its inhabitants. In each grain of sand, each leaf and bud, is the pattern of creation and the Creator. If one would like to know the heavens, first learn about Gaia ("as above, so below," the saying goes).

When it comes to animals, many of us have pets and work as animal advocates. Some of these creatures are far more than simple household features—they've become spiritual guides and helpmates. The stories in this chapter share from the domains of nature and the animal kingdom.

ENCOUNTERING THE DIVINE IN NATURE

PHYLLIS CUROTT

Nature is the embodiment of divinity. Indigenous peoples lived close to the land and therefore saw the natural world as holy. If you're like me, you live much of your life largely separated from Nature, and so you and I must work harder to establish this sacred and magickal relationship. But the rewards are well worth the effort.

One of the old definitions of a Witch was someone who works with hidden or unseen forces. In a sense that's true—you can't see subatomic particles, nor can you see the waves of energy at the heart of those particles, but you do see the material expression of that energy. Just as seeing someone smile is seeing the outer and physical expression of her or his inner emotional (or energetic) life, when you see the Earth in all of its perfect and balanced beauty, you are looking at the outer expression of an inner divinity.

In fact, I have a new definition of a Witch: a Witch is someone who is paying attention, who is aware of the divine Presence in all things. And if you are seeking the sacred, you will find it by immersing yourself in Nature. Nature makes the divine tangible. Nature is the gown the

Goddess wears to make herself visible, and the dance the God dances to express his joy. Looking at Nature, we see living, incarnate divinity.

Yet so much of our magick is made indoors—in our houses or apartments, and in our imaginations on transcendental or akashic planes. We visualize being in a spring meadow, or sitting beneath a towering oak, or circling in a sacred forest glade. We imagine traveling to power places on the astral plane. Much of this mental work is an inheritance from our ceremonial magician forebears, whose concepts of magick were deeply influenced by biblical theology and patriarchal culture. Although they were certainly among their culture's avant-garde and strongly influenced by the Romantic era, which embraced Nature, they were also products of their own Victorian culture, in which the desires of the body were largely suppressed and denied, so they confined most of their magick to the head.

The common approach to Witchcraft, and to making magick, is to imagine the Air, the Water, the Sun, the Earth. But magick can't just be imagined, it has to be felt, and lived, and embodied. You don't need to imagine divinity when you are standing in the midst of a redwood forest, or diving with ancient tortoises near the Great Barrier Reef, or helping to harvest a field of golden corn, or dancing naked beneath a full moon. You can feel it with every fiber of your being. And so, whenever possible, you should perform your magickal and ritual practices outdoors—cast a circle under the moon's light, ground and center in a forest clearing, purify in the sea. We make the best magick in Nature because Nature makes the best magick. Nature *is* magick, because it is the body of the Divine. And Nature's magick doesn't have to be imagined, it just has to be experienced.

I'll never forget one of my earliest lessons on getting out of my head and into Nature. It was March, just a few days before the spring equinox, and I decided to do some spring cleaning—with magick. I cleaned out my closets and scrubbed my apartment until it shone. I even did my taxes. I took sage and salt water and moved widdershins (counterclockwise—the direction of banishing) all around the edge of the apartment. I opened the windows and the front door and I swept out all the stale energy of winter. But there were still some cobwebs—in me!

So I got in my car and drove to one of my favorite natural spots, the Delaware Water Gap. I hiked into the still-barren woods, astonished at how soft and soggy the land was. Every time I saw a tiny shoot of green poking through the ground, I felt happier and more optimistic. The snows had melted, and the runoff from the ridges had filled the streams with rushing water.

My plan was to wash my hair under a tiny waterfall in one of the streams I often visited. The air was crisp and exhilarating as I scrambled along the bank of the stream. I carefully worked my way up to a small "waterfall" about eighteen inches wide. The sound of the water was wonderful and hypnotic as I stared into the tumbling cascade. I took off my coat, pulled off my sweater, and carefully leaned forward, sticking my head into the water. I was stunned: the water was freezing cold and hit me with the force of a sledgehammer! I gasped for breath as it ripped all thought, all worry, all intention from my mind. I pulled myself from the stream, grabbing for my towel and collapsing against the damp earth. I have never in my life been so utterly, ecstatically clear. It sure beat politely dipping my fingers in a dainty bowl of salt water back in my newly cleaned apartment.

Nature knows how to make magick, and it's more than willing to teach us. Because it is the embodiment of the Divine, Nature is our greatest spiritual teacher. When the student is ready, the teacher will appear. Practitioners of Earth religions, such as modern Witchcraft, are students of Nature's wisdom, and your teacher—Nature—is always available. Though we may not have ancient books of wisdom or an unbroken line of traditions, we have the same teacher that our forebears learned from. And even if all you have is a small city park to walk in, or a plant on your windowsill, Nature is present if you'll just pay attention.

What will it teach you? The answer depends on how you approach being taught. What mind-set, emotional framework, and posture will you take? The old relationship of imposing our will on Nature, whether we use magick or technology, doesn't serve anyone; in fact, it only sep-arates us from Nature and from the Divine. Most of our problems come from this separation, for to be cut off from Nature is to be cut off from divinity. Just as we need the Earth in order to live physically—for food, air, water, and countless other blessings—we need the Earth if we are to live spiritually.

Physics has taught us that what you bring to the experiment affects the outcome. So when you approach Nature as your spiritual teacher, you need to be open, receptive, attentive, deferential, and appreciative. This is the "right relationship" Native Americans and Buddhists refer to—it is based on attentiveness to the divinity of Nature, respect, and gratitude. The activity below is an innovative magickal practice that is not just for beginners, but is especially for veteran practitioners who have mastered the arts of changing consciousness at will using mental skills. This is a practice that will ground your magick in your body and the Earth, and will greatly enhance your experience and your results wherever you work, indoors or out.

sensitivity training

Our culture is very busy, and making a quick transition to a meditative state in a natural environment is not always easy. Physical activity—such as hiking, working in your garden, cleaning up the natural area you are going to work in—can help you relax and focus. It will also help you reap the magic that paying attention provides. You may wish to tape this exercise so you can listen to it while you prepare.

After you have done some moderate, comfortable physical exercise, such as walking or stretching, find an attractive natural setting that appeals to you. It can be your backyard, a local park, a wilderness trail, or other outdoor location. Find a "power spot"—a place that gives you a positive feeling, or where you receive a visible sign, such as an animal appearing and not being disturbed by your presence.

Ask the spot's permission to work with it. It's good to pick a place that you can come back to because each time you work with it, the place will become more powerful for you, and you in turn will contribute to its well-being. How long you practice the exercise is up to you—it depends on your attention span and your feelings as you remain in the spot, but ten minutes is a good length of time. The goal is to isolate one of your senses, and then to concentrate on it, paying attention to your experience of the natural environment you have chosen.

Sit down, close your eyes, breathe deeply, and clear your mind of wandering thoughts. Now bring your attention back to your body. Notice how you are feeling—are you cold, hot, uncomfortable sitting on the ground? And now bring your attention to one of your senses and what it is experiencing. Begin by listening to the sounds carried by the air. Remain still and really listen. What do you hear? Are you hearing distracting sounds such as traffic, machinery, airplanes, or the voices of other people? I live in the country, but there is almost always a background hum of human sounds, even late at night.

You may have difficulty finding a place that is free from noise pollution, but we can learn even from that. If there is indeed a background hum of humanity, listen to what the sounds are, where they come from, and most important, how they make you feel. Now open your eyes and look around you. Enjoy the beauty of the spot.

When you feel ready, close your eyes again, and this time focus on the natural sounds of the setting you have chosen. Let go of any distracting noise pollution, just as you learned to let distracting thoughts float by when you meditate. Focus on the natural sounds, and keep your eyes closed while you listen carefully. What do you hear? A bird? Several birds? A flock? Where are they? Are they talking to each other, as crows do? Are they singing? How do their songs make you feel? Do you hear the wind blowing, leaves rustling, trees whispering? Do you hear dogs barking? Do you hear insects, bees, frogs? Are you hearing sounds you never noticed before? How do you feel?

Listen to the silence between sounds. If your mind starts to wander, you can return to being present in the moment by again focusing on the sounds of Nature. When you're ready, open your eyes. See if you can spot the sources of your sounds. Do you know what made the sounds? How does listening to Nature make you feel? You may wish to write down how you felt and what you experienced in your magickal journal. Try to return to this spot at different times of the day, and at night (if it is safe to do so), and during different seasons. Pay attention to the differences in what you hear, and feel, on these occasions.

In the future, when you return to this spot or repeat this exercise of attentive listening, you may hear a song or poem within you. When you do this exercise again, you may wish to begin by singing or reciting your inspiration. Be sure to thank the place, and your companions. This Sensitivity Training exercise can, and should, be used to develop your other senses as well. For sight, notice all the details you can; for smell, concentrate on the scents around you; and so on. Try each sense's exercise again at a different time of day, or in a different season, and notice what changes. As you learn to focus your attention, your senses—sight, sound, taste, touch, smell, intuition, and other natural senses that we have all neglected, living in an overcivilized world—will become keener and more aware. By paying careful attention to our teacher, Nature, you are beginning to attune yourself to its rhythm, to the sacred wisdom in its flow of energy. Nature is crafting you as a Witch. It's so delightful to live in a magickal world!

As I am writing this, I hear an unfamiliar bird in the still, winter afternoon air. I just opened my door to see two woodpeckers exploring one of the weeping birch trees in the front yard. They are rare and wonderful visitors—so I send you their greetings and encouragement!

—Phyllis Curott—

EARTH RELIGION IN THE MODERN WORLD

EARTHWIZARD

A dear friend of mine asked me a series of simple questions the other day: "You always speak of the Old Religion of the Earth as if it were something that everyone should know exists. So tell me: What exactly is this Old Religion? Does it have a founder, like the religions of Buddhism, Judaism, Christianity, and Islam? When did it begin? Does it have a literature? And one more thing: What impact for good or ill has it had on your personal life? Has it helped you survive the daily onslaught of the world?"

Boy, was I astounded. Here was a close friend who had known me for many years, even though we have had to continue our friendship by phone because of work changes and lifestyles. And she had never asked me these kinds of questions before. She'd just accepted me for who I was. Now she was seeking answers—trying to understand exactly what it was this Old Religion of the Earth represented, who were its authorities and spokespersons, and what it had to offer her that other religions didn't already offer. Did it have a literature: a bible, an explicatory and expository canon, a tradition of poets, artists, writers who have come

down to us from antiquity like the traditions of the Western canon? All
of these are good questions, and to tell the truth, I was taken aback:
I didn't have any clear-cut answers for her. I described the only essential
truth that I could relate: the Old Religion is real for me because I have
felt the presence of the Goddess in my personal life. But how could
I translate that feeling into something rational, explain it with words that
would truly cross the divide of our disparate cultures and have meaning
in the context of our world's social, economic, political, religious, and
cultural mind-sets?

Language sunders us from ourselves; it wanders among meanings
like a lost tribe of elves, seeking the lands of youth, wandering through
time picking up stories and tales of wonder along the way, but never
coming to the final destination: home. I was dumbfounded, could not
come up with a rational set of beliefs to give her beyond the typical
shibboleths of the tradition I'd learned ages ago in my early apprentice-
ship into the Wiccan tradition of modern Witchcraft. I could not tell her
that we had a founder like the Buddha, Moses, Abraham, Jesus, Muhammad.
Our way is different: we do not have prophets or religious founders.
But we do have poets, dreamers, visionaries; myths, legends, tales, and
poems. Our tradition was essentially hidden; it had been forced to go
underground because of those very powerful religions of the "one true
God," who through all ages was a jealous god who would have no other
before him. All the monotheistic faiths have seemed unable to accept
a pluralistic worldview; they have sought unity, a framework based on
hierarchy with God at the top and all others under his tutelage and
command. Can anyone say why this came about? Does anyone truly
have an answer?

I've pondered these questions for thirty years and still only grasp
certain definable truths. Like many other men in this Western cultural
complex that is America, I was raised with Christian values and beliefs.
But in my case there was one difference: my mother hid her true self,
her essential beliefs, her knowledge of the old ways that had been
passed down to her by the elder women in our clan. She'd come out of
old Pennsylvanian stock, had been raised with cunning women and men
who knew the secret byways of the earth, soil, and land. They were

farmers and crafters, skilled in the old ways of earth and tribe, their ancient German heritage shining through clearly and distinctly in the ethic of hard work, social gatherings at the stations of the farming year, planting by the moon, and living with a deep knowledge of the traditions of their forebears reaching back into a dim age. These were people who had earned their way by hand to mouth—pragmatic learning shaped by an agricultural worldview that is now almost gone from our country (thanks to the giant mega farming machines of our era; but that is another tale).

I remember the first time I was touched by the power of magick. As a child, we used to gather and play games at the family table to pass the time during the long winters. One night my mother told us a story that her great-aunt had told her long ago.

Once upon a time in an age before our age, a woman lived at the edge of a dark forest full of wolves, and bears, and all things wild. She had a daughter whose name was Altheia, who would wander alone in the woods unafraid of beast or man.

One day this little girl happened on a little man who was sitting by a stream, as if pondering the deepest mysteries of the universe. He did not look up as the little girl approached; yet he spoke softly to her, without ever turning his head: "Oh, so you have come at last. Now that you are here, you can begin gathering fruit for my basket." The little girl laughed, astonished to see such a little man dressed in red and green and golden cloth, his eyes full of gleeful mischief, his great frizz of yellow hair flowing round his shoulders, and a blue cap with a white feather rising out of it like some beautiful and exotic bird.

The little girl answered the wee man like this: "I'm sorry, but I do not have any fruit to fill your basket. There is no fruit in this forest but the blackberries and wild strawberries, which the great black bear eats for his pleasure during the late summer." And the little man looked up at last, with a wee winkle in his eye, laughing, and said, "Oh, but there is, my dear; for I know a tree hidden in the center of the forest that bears a special fruit." The little girl looked quizzically at him and smiled, saying, "And perchance, will you show me this wondrous tree and its fruit?" The wee man laughed again, got up from his toadstool, and proceeded to walk off down a dark path deeper and deeper into the forest. Not a word did he speak to the little girl, but began singing a little ditty, an old tune full of light and the sun's laughter. The little girl stood there perplexed for a moment, and then followed the wee man into the dark forest.

They walked for some time. She watched the little man intently as he hopped and skipped, sang and danced to his tunes of merriment. And before long they entered a large clearing at the center of the forest that was surrounded by huge oaks and willows and wild thickets full of thorns and nettles.

This was no ordinary place, the little girl felt; she knew instinctively that it was a place of magick, full of mystery and strange music. Yet she felt at home in this wild place, felt that for the first time in her life she was in the presence of a power that was in harmony with her own wild and untamed nature. She began to laugh and dance around the green ring that bordered the great temple of trees. She felt all warm and alive inside, as if she were sitting by the cozy hearth in her mother's home. She felt at peace with all living things.

She continued to dance around and around the bright green ring until she suddenly saw a little white tree at the center of the clearing. She could see bright red fruit hanging down from its branches, within easy reach of her little hands. She ran up and plucked a juicy red morsel and bit into it so quickly that the wee man, who had been watching her all this time from a distance, was unable to speak quickly enough to dissuade her from such a foolish act. However, the deed was done; there was no turning back. She stood there smiling, full of the wild pulp of this soft and fleshy fruit, letting its juices dribble down her soft cheek onto her clean white dress. It didn't matter to her; she was so full of wonder and bliss that nothing would ever bother her again.

Then it happened. One moment she was standing there alone with the wee man in the green ring at the center of the deep wild wood enjoying bliss, the next she heard the laughter of the others.

She stopped chewing on the bright red fruit and looked around her. What she saw was amazing. Dancing and prancing with laughter and glee were the smallest people she'd ever seen. And at the center of the ring stood the wee little man, their king. He looked at her with a stern eye, then smiled in merriment, saying, "Well now, my little one, you have come home to us again from your travels in the world of men. Now you must choose: to stay or go back to the world of men. Do not choose too quickly, little one, for your choice will have lasting repercussions. For you see, we are the little people, the fair folk, and we live in the wild woods protecting all natural things from the onslaught of men who would destroy the Earth and her children of the forest, glen, and deep woods. And, you, my dear, are one of our progeny—a changeling left at the door of men to grow among them and show them the ways of our queen, the White Lady of the Forest."

The little girl was not surprised. She felt something stir in her inner self, a deep echo of acknowledgment, a recognition: "Yes, I am an elven queen." She knew innately what she must do, and spoke thus: "I will return to the world of men. I will teach them the ways of the fair folk—show them the natural ways of Earth, Water, Fire, and Air; open their minds to the old ways of our kind. Some will listen and tell others. Yes, some will even begin to realize that they too are changelings lost among the dark hollows of this bright Earth, their deeper selves unknown, asleep. Yes, I must awaken them from their long sleep and give them back the dream of Earth. Teach them the ways of the Goddess, our mother."

The King of the Elves laughed in glee as the little girl disappeared from view, going back into the world of men with the good news that the old ways of the Earth are still alive and full of magic, ritual, joy, and mystery.

When my mother finished this tale, I remember feeling something stir deep inside me. Something was awakening for the first time in long time: a sleeping self at the center of my being had suddenly opened his eyes from a long sleep. From that moment on I began a quest to understand this deep heritage of our ancient guardians of the wild places. And my secret companion has been with me ever since.

> May the Goddess find you healthy.
> May she bless you with plenty.
> May her magick touch your life forever.

MAN'S BEST FRIEND

KRISTIN MADDEN

"Man's best friend" is a very special being, and this piece is dedicated to one special friend in particular. Cosmo, the big white dog, brought joy, love, and companionship to Sandy, a treasured member of my magickal community. Cosmo's illness pulled our community together in support of him and his human. Because of him, we learned what we can accomplish when we come together and Sandy received back some of the tremendous amount of energy she has put into our community over the years. Few animals can give that kind of loyal service. Dog is one who truly can.

When we think of pets as spirit guides, most people think only of cats. Dogs are silly, goofy, lovable animals and can be great protectors, but few of us think of them as powerful beings of spirit. Like many "pet" animals, dogs have a way of plugging right into our heart chakra. We are allowed to be our true selves with dogs, and they encourage us to be playful, silly, emotional, affectionate, and all those things we can be when we need no walls up for protection.

Dogs held special positions of honor among several ancient and indigenous peoples. Because of their reputations as courageous guardians, the term meaning "dog," *Cú,* became a title of honor among the ancient Celts. The names of many heroes, warriors, and chiefs were preceded by this honorific, including the great hero of Ulster, Cú Chulainn. Dogs bring the medicine of true and loyal friendship, of bravery and protection. Their unconditional love has the potential to spur us into becoming the wonderful beings they see in us.

While all dogs share this general Dog medicine, each breed and individual will bring in more specific energies. My chow-Akita holds a very different energy for me than my Old English sheepdog did, or my German shepherd. This is something every dog person needs to uncover through developing that relationship.

People with Dog medicine are often of service to their communities as healers, counselors, or organizers. Like wolves, dogs are pack animals, and the good of the pack supersedes that of the individual. These people do not set themselves up as celebrities, nor do they demand that others conform to their way of living. They do their work without concern for what they will get in return. Their greatest payment is not fame or fortune, but the love of community and the knowledge that they have done something good.

Dog medicine people will take a great deal of abuse before they suffer enough wounding to retaliate. They continue to offer love in the face of abuse. This shows us the depth of their compassion and understanding of how our shadows influence our behavior. But even Dog people will not tolerate bad treatment forever. If you are lucky, they will simply leave the relationship. But when a dog turns, it can be a truly frightening experience. Dog nature may ask us to be more forgiving or more understanding of the faults of others; on the other hand, it may call us to be less submissive and to learn to stand up for ourselves.

Dogs are also the guardians of the crossroads and the gateway to the Otherworlds, particularly the Lowerworld. Just as our dogs guide and protect us in this realm, so do they walk with us on our journeys to other realms. Dog is a wonderful journeying companion, especially for children or anyone new to conscious out-of-body travel. This is a friend you can rely on in all worlds.

canine connection spell

Try this simple spell to deepen your connection and open the doors of non-verbal communication between you and your dog. Allow a bowl of water to charge with the energy of both sun and moon. Holding the bowl at your forehead with both hands, close your eyes and visualize yourself with your pet. Evoke the love you feel for this animal. See yourself in telepathic communication with your pet. You intuitively understand each other. Feel your bond of love and respect deepen. Send these images and feelings into the water.

Pour half of this water into your dog's bowl and drink the other half yourself. Chant this as you pour and drink:

> Blessed Water, open the way
> To greater love and understanding today
> For now and future days to come
> Bless us now, make us one.

Afterward, spend some time with your dog. Clear your mind of any thoughts or worries and focus your full attention on your appreciation of this being and your relationship. Be aware of any messages or feelings that come through at this time. Continue to spend this time regularly, at least until you recognize the effects of the spell.

—Kristin Madden—

FURRY FRIENDS:
TEACHING ONLINE

BRANWEN

Although I've taught students and led groups occasionally, my primary Pagan teaching in recent years has been as the webmistress of a Pagan website. My principal interaction with the community is thus faceless and somewhat impersonal. The site has a message board frequented by many regular participants, whom I sometimes consider my students, sometimes my teachers, and always my friends, though we actually know little about one another. Teaching in this context requires a good bit of confidence in one's area of expertise, along with communication skills and a commitment to the issues involved.

While the message board is open to all areas of Pagan discussion, I'm most at home in the "Furry Friends" forum. My goal there is to lead by providing a place for advice—either from myself or from others—on animal care and, more generally, on ways to connect with Nature in one's spiritual path. This forum started quite naturally when I wrote about my pets now and then. Since we also use the forum to request energy for healing, I asked participants to send energy to the kittens I foster for Kitten Rescue. Soon people wanted to know more about my rescue work, and as I talked about it I was reminded of some of the projects I'd required from students in the past.

When I was teaching, my students were aware that for me, an Earth-centered path means more than acknowledging the changing seasons and the phases of the moon. It is literally a path that comes from the Earth and is bound to it, not only by a spiritual link but through practical and productive activity. Thus it was no surprise to them when I required them as part of their training to create or participate in a project that aided the environment or the Earth's inhabitants.

The projects varied as people's skills varied. Organizations that help protect the environment or aid animals need people with a great many skills. They need people to work on fund-raising, to organize political actions, and in recent years to create and maintain websites, to name just a few. Of course, they also need people who can work directly with animals, doing jobs ranging from cleaning cages to reintroducing wildlife to the natural habitat. I tried to teach students that no job was too small or too menial if the result was to contribute something to the Earth. Also, no job was too removed from the Earth to help create a spiritual bond.

As my students were usually from urban areas, their projects were generally of two types. Some joined organizations and offered their time for office work of various kinds. Others took a more hands-on approach, volunteering to foster homeless animals and perform other tasks in animal rescue organizations. Since I have rescued cats for most of my life, I could easily help students get involved in either cat or dog rescue in the city through the various connections I had with these organizations.

This kind of teaching was much more direct than what I do now. I knew the organizations that could help students get started. When they fostered animals, I could check on them to see how things were going. Most important, we had many conversations about why we should do these things, what such actions mean in terms of spirituality, and how we can serve the gods in the future. Now I use the "Furry Friends" forum of my message board to try to teach the same things. For example, someone asked about declawing cats, and this query started a lengthy thread discussing not just this procedure but also our responsibilities toward animals. If I'm going to post an answer in such a thread, I don't just go with whatever anecdotal information I have on the subject.

I generally do some research in the veterinary journals, talk to trusted vets, and look at the studies done on the procedure and its effects. People are expecting me to know something about it, not just sound off, and sometimes they are getting their first pet and really need the answers. Many other participants add their knowledge, both from personal experience and from their research. Taking the declawing thread as an example, most people came away convinced that the procedure is risky to a pet and that there are other means of reducing the damage a cat may cause (training, regular claw trimming, claw caps, and so on).

Aside from the medical issues involved in declawing, there is also a spiritual issue in the sense that the way we treat animals demonstrates our reverence, or lack of it, for the Earth. If we respect the Earth's creatures, then we have no right to alter them surgically solely for our benefit, whether it's to protect our belongings or to win awards in shows, as in the case of ear or tail cropping of some dog breeds. Animals should be allowed to be what they are, what Nature made them, not changed according to our preferences.

One might wonder then about the spiritual ethics of spaying and neutering. Humans abandon animals to breed in areas where food and shelter are insufficient and where they are often killed as pests for searching for food near homes. Since we are responsible for the overpopulation, we are also responsible for controlling it. A person who believes that it is wrong to alter a dog or cat but doesn't take responsibility for securing good homes for their offspring isn't doing the animals any favors. Finding plastic bags of dead or dying kittens and puppies in garbage bins year after year is pretty good evidence that sterilization benefits the animals. As spiritual people and caretakers of this planet, it's important that we think a situation through to the end result.

The topics in the "Furry Friends" forum cover many subjects, and thus offer many ways for Pagans to get involved in helping animals, including pets. A healthy and happy pet teaches what is necessary and valuable in life. Surely everyone has seen joyous dogs and contented cats and wished to be so at peace with the world. Animals have valuable lessons to teach us, and we are perfectly placed to observe our own pets. They need food and water, shelter, medical care when necessary, and love. Do we really need more?

pet protection

Not everyone can volunteer to work with animals, but that doesn't mean you can't help. Be informed and involved. Rescue organizations and no-kill shelters need money, and they need publicity. There is always something that needs to be done in these areas, whether it's staffing a donation booth at an event or posting a banner on a website.

Most of all, rescue groups need public policies that are favorable to the safety of all our natural resources as well as our abandoned animals. Find out what the candidates in your region think about animal welfare policies, and vote for the ones who favor humane treatment for all animals. This is especially important at the local level, where a city council can quickly make a decision affecting thousands of animals. If you aren't old enough to vote, do the same research and then volunteer to help in a candidate's campaign.

I used the spells below together in a protection ritual for a house and its inhabitants, including the pets. In both spells, Hecate is called on for her fierce protective attributes. I've explained the circumstances in each case, but you would want to make changes to fit the circumstances and characteristics of your pets.

To protect a dog: The dog I wanted to protect is a beautiful, loving pet. He is also a pit bull and very protective of his family. My fear has always been that by protecting them from intruders or other harm, he would later be harmed himself because of the fear many people have of the breed.

Call your dog into the circle and draw a pentagram in protection oil (or any blessing oil you like) on his forehead. Then recite,

Hecate, Dark Mother
In protecting this home

In your place as is right
Stands one of your own

In defending this house
And all creatures within
Your sacred beast
Is your true loyal friend.

Keep him from harm
As he guards all he loves
And watch over him
So below, as above.

To protect a cat: The cat in this case had just moved into a new house. He kept running away every time a door or window was opened.

Call your cat into the circle and draw a pentagram in protection oil on his forehead. Then recite,

Moon Goddess, I ask
That you keep this cat at home
And safe from his mischief
And desire to roam.

Give him the contentment
Known to his race
And see that he's happy
In this his new place.

Perform these tasks in the Goddess's name. She is Earth. She is Nature. She is the Source of us all and what sustains us. Surely the Goddess rewards those who have compassion for her children.

—Branwen—

NATURE'S SENSE OF HUMOR

MARIAN SINGER

There are moments in life when one would swear that the entire Earth giggles. One such occasion happened for me several years ago at an outdoor festival. The ritual had just come to an end, and we all found ourselves milling around the ritual fires, chatting merrily. The stars were crystal clear overhead, and the scent of spring floated gently on the air. This made for a lovely setting, except for the fact that there was nowhere to sit but the ground, and when you have back problems that's not such a good idea (getting down isn't so bad, it's getting back up that's difficult).

Rather than get stuck, I decided just to stretch out. Mind you, I was wearing a long flowing cloak, carrying a walking stick in one hand and a goblet in the other. I stretched my hands up to the sky. At just that moment, an air pocket in the ritual fire exploded with a resounding crackle. Sparks flew in all directions, lighting up the darkness. The gentleman next to me looked at the fire, looked at my arms, and commented without missing a beat, "Hey, not bad!" We both laughed, and the salamanders laughed with us. Even in nature, timing is everything.

Tickling Your Aura

The Universe has a sense of humor. If you haven't tickled your funny bone lately, remember that laughter is good for the soul. One way to cheer up a bad case of the blues is by tickling your aura.

For this you'll need a feather, some lighthearted incense (your choice), and a few minutes of quiet. Light the incense. Focus on any negativity or stress you might be carrying and let it drain out of your feet into the floor. Stomp on it! Be firm! Have fun! Once you've stomped it silly, take the feather in one hand and the incense in the other and smudge your aura: use the feather to waft the incense smoke all around you, saying,

> Joy be quick, laughter be kind
> Awaken and lighten my weighed-down mind!

Repeat the incantation until you've finished smudging, then go rent a comedy video or do something that empowers your inner child.

—Marian Singer—

THE RIVER

OBERON ZELL-RAVENHEART

For eleven years of my later life (the longest time ever spent in one home), I lived with my expanded family (Morning Glory, Diane, Bryan, Rainbow, Zack, Gary, Wynter) right on the Rushing River (or *Russian River,* as it was called by mundanes), in Mendocino County, NorCalifia. We called our home the Old Same Place, after a line from a Firesign Theater skit ("Nick Danger: Third Eye"). Our backyard was a private beach and swimming hole, with a rope swing dangling from a high tree. Salmon, trout, and otters played in the running waters; ospreys, kingfishers, and herons fished from above; deer and raccoons visited at night; and beloved friends hung out all the time.

At the beginning of each summer, I would go to a tire store and buy up a bunch of used but airtight truck inner tubes. On many weekends, especially at the Sabbats of Litha (summer solstice) and Lughnasadh (Lammas), we would gather up a bunch of folks and tubes, take everyone a few miles upstream in trucks, and float down the river back to our place—or sometimes much farther, all the way to Lake Mendocino, another two miles downstream. Depending on their length, these trips would take from two to four hours.

Along the way, the experience itself offered so many lessons that I came to think of it as a magickal teaching all its own, and I presented it so to all those I introduced to the river. There were rapids with white water; deep, still pools for swimming; giant rocks forming narrow passages; tall rocks to jump from; lushly overgrown little islands; sandy beaches and gravel bars; thickets of delicious ripe blackberries overhanging the banks. Sunlight dappled through the leaves of the trees along each side, providing a perfect mix of sun and shade. Ours was the only habitation along these stretches, and we would see no other people or signs of civilization—we might as well have been in a remote jungle. Often, as we rounded a turn, we would come upon deer drinking at the clear water.

Drifting along, arms and legs draped over the sides of the tube, embraced by the arms of the river nymphs, and watching the world go by, has been the most peaceful, perfect place I have ever known for meditation and reflection. The more times we rode down that river (and, of course, I went far more often than anyone else), the better we would get at navigating it. By coming to know the river, I now *know* rivers, and I can tube, raft, canoe, or kayak along them with perfect ease. I have even done serious white-water rafting down a world-class river in Costa Rica.

Here are some of the best lessons I've learned from the river:

1. *The stream of consciousness flows like a river.* Spirit moves like water. It's always seeking to return to the Source, and it always finds its own level. Like water, Spirit can be bottled up, diverted, or dammed for a time. But eventually the container will break and water/spirit will flow free and move to continue its passage downstream. Water/spirit diverted will find a way around, cutting new channels to rejoin its course. Dams will one day overflow and be swept away, and the flow will continue, always toward the ocean whence it came. As water flows ever downward to merge with the vast ocean below, Spirit flows ever upward to merge with the eternal cosmic Ocean above.

2. *Go with the flow.* Anytime you come to a fork in the river, a big rock in the way, a logjam, an island, or rapids ahead—and you can't see ahead to know which passage to take—the trick is to

study the current. Wherever the current is strongest, there will be a V in the water, and all you have to do is steer your tube down the center of the V. Trusting the flow rather than fighting it, you become one with the current, which will carry you around and over all obstacles. But often newbies try to paddle desperately to avoid the fast water, and they find themselves getting swept into rocks, logs, and embankments—or just going around and around in a little side eddy and left behind by the rest of us. Just so in life: The trick is to learn to see the flow of the current and then steer your course right into the middle of it. The heart of the flow may seem too fast and scary, but it is truly the safest course.

3. You can *change the course of mighty rivers with your bare hands.* Every river begins with a tiny stream. If you go far enough back upstream toward the source, the course of that stream can be changed by moving only a few pebbles. Farther down, it takes boulders; and far enough along, whole mountains would have to be moved. In the streams of consciousness, I've moved plenty of pebbles in my time—and even quite a number of boulders— and I've diverted tiny rivulets that have become mighty, raging torrents, which in turn have carved great canyons and washed away mountains.

Consciousness, like water, ultimately cannot be resisted, and through dark times, I draw my hope and inspiration from this certainty.

going with the flow

Take an inner-tube trip. Find a river or large stream somewhere you can get to easily that is suitable for inner-tubing in the summer. You may have to ask around a bit. It should be not so small that the water doesn't flow, or it's too shallow to float in; and not so big or fast as to be dangerous. Ideal rivers for kayaking are often also good for tubing, as long as there's enough of a current to carry you along.

Get some friends—including at least one with experience—who'd like to make a day of tubing. Get truck inner tubes and overinflate them into the shape of a fat donut. Wear sneakers or good rubber sandals that won't come off in the water. Practice maneuvering in a still pool before you venture into the moving water. If you should capsize, hold on to your tube! You'll need a big pickup truck to carry yourselves and your tubes to the upstream drop-off place, and someone who will drive down to the other end to pick you up.

Start with a short, easy trip—maybe a mile or so—and try longer ones as you get better at it. Go with the flow, and become one with the cosmic stream of consciousness . . .

—Oberon Zell-Ravenheart—

WEATHER MAGICK

Janina Renée

Many societies recognize a special relationship between frogs and rain. Thus in times of drought in India, some villagers will make an effigy of a frog and sprinkle it with water while singing songs begging the rain to have pity on the frogs; and in the movie *The Emerald Forest,* the hero implores the frogs to sing very loudly to bring on a massive downpour. Some other societies' rainmaking ceremonies involve sprinkling water on special rainstones, or on other people.

When California was suffering from a drought back in the early nineties, I guided my little group in a ceremony to which I brought a Play-Doh relief map of California (which my son had made for a school project), a large Mexican silver frog belonging to my mother, a bunch of plastic flipping frogs, and a number of polished malachite and aventurine gemstones. We then arranged the frogs and stones on the map and around the altar, and danced about as we sprinkled everything and everyone with water; we also flipped the plastic frogs back and forth. (It did rain shortly thereafter.)

Then, about a week ago, my farmer neighbors mentioned that they were worried about the soybean crop, because Michigan (where I now live) has been experiencing a drought. So I got out a little green quartz frog pendant and sprinkled it, and we did have quite a heavy downpour at the beginning of this week. A good (and fun) rainmaking chant is:

Rain, rain, come today,
All your froggies want to play.

This sort of ceremony could be incorporated into a community festival too.

Rain Rituals

Here are a few wise-woman methods for bringing rain:

- Dipping a broom in water and shaking it out on the ground
- Placing green jade in a bowl of water outside
- Making weather knots (loosening only one at a time, as needed)
- Releasing a water-oriented flower (such as a lily) into a moving water source flowing in the direction you want the rain to go

—Patricia Telesco—

THE SNAKESKIN

JENNIE DUNHAM

In our backyard we have a series of steps made out of large wooden railroad ties. They have probably been there since the house was built more than twenty years ago, and like everything about our house, the steps are getting a bit worn. There is a crevice in the third step, and an ordinary garter snake lives there. We know this because the snake occasionally comes out to lie in the sun, and if one of us happens to walk up the steps, the snake slips back into its home.

Last summer my husband, Craig, picked me up at the train station after I'd had a long day at work, and he said he'd found a surprise. He took me to the steps, and there I saw what he'd found. He hadn't touched it yet. The snake had shed its skin, and Craig had saved it for me. I was seven months pregnant at the time, and he wanted me to have it.

"It's still wet," he said.

"And it's whole. The head and tail are intact," I replied. It was the snake's gift to us.

Snakeskin in hand, I now had some serious thinking ahead of me. I brought the gift to my altar and placed it there. I sat quietly with it in front of me. Snakeskin represents change in the grand sense of transformation, shedding the old and replacing it with the new. This kind of change was ahead of me as I prepared to become a mother.

But let me be honest here: I hated being pregnant. I threw up again and again. I felt awful day in and day out. There was nothing "morning" about the morning sickness I experienced. I couldn't sleep well. No position seemed comfortable, and I kept waking up. I couldn't eat much, and twice my weight went down during the pregnancy. Despite the loving care Craig gave me throughout, I wished I wasn't pregnant. Feeling guilty and worried about it, I even asked my midwife if any new moms took out their resentment about their pregnancies on their new babies.

And beyond all that discomfort loomed the agony of labor and delivery. We'd chosen natural childbirth classes, which seemed the best method of giving our baby a good start. And we planned on giving birth in the comfortable environment of a birthing center to avoid the hospital, though one was close by in case of an emergency. But how would I get through the pain of labor? All I could think was that feeling miserable during the pregnancy would be nothing compared to what I'd face during labor and delivery.

This is how I realized that I should save the snakeskin for the birth. I left it on my altar in the remaining weeks. The saying I created to accompany the snakeskin was "a safe and easy birth," and I would carry that image and saying with me almost as a talisman and good luck charm to keep in mind firmly as I visualized the natural birth Craig and I wanted.

Two weeks before my due date, I went to the midwife's office on a Friday for a routine check. She wanted to make sure I didn't have preeclampsia, because of a sharp increase in weight gain and water retention. I felt no worse than I had for months, and her concern seemed pretty bogus to me, but I was willing to have the nonstress test to prove that I should wait for labor to start naturally.

To my dismay, the midwife confirmed that I did have preeclampsia and would need to go to the hospital right away to have labor induced. Everything I didn't want was becoming a reality. I was furious at her insistence that I go to the hospital: that was supposed to be for emergencies only. And how would I avoid medication with the increased pain of forced labor? I knew now that I would break down and ask for an epidural. My baby would just have to get over it.

Was our nursery ready? No, it had yellow walls but no crib or rocking chair. Was our hospital bag packed? No, we thought we still had two weeks to go. Craig ran around the house ripping tags off baby clothes so that our wee one would have something to wear home. He packed food so that we could snack during our hospital stay, and he sorted through clothes for both of us. I called my family to alert them, and then I set about packing a small altar with a crystal athame, a twig wand, a glass for water, and a container of salt. I packed a pumpkin spice–scented candle to honor the October birth. Last of all I delicately coiled the dry snakeskin around the other items in our portable altar box.

I can honestly say that we are the only people who have ever brought a snakeskin into Danbury Hospital.

Friday afternoon the midwife inserted the first suppository to get labor started. I lay in the bed, but nothing happened. Three hours later it was evening and I received another dose, but nothing happened. Three more hours later it was night and I received a third dose, but nothing happened. My midwife sent my family home, saying that labor had not begun and that there was no need for them to wait expectantly. She'd just keep the suppositories coming until contractions started.

We turned off the lights to darken the room, but I had way too much energy to sleep as I dreaded another dose of medicine. About 1:00 A.M. Craig fell asleep in some contorted position on the couch, so I asked a nurse to keep me company and talk to me quietly. She told me that my midwife had had another client come in who was close to delivery, so she would skip my next dose of induction medicine. I told the nurse that I was angry at being in the hospital, frustrated at having an induction I didn't want, and worried about the pain I'd feel once labor did get going.

"Nobody ever died of pain," she said calmly. Somehow she seemed right about that.

"I'm making it harder for myself than I need to," I said. "If I accepted my situation and tried to work with it, I know I'd be better off. Fighting against it will only delay the birth and increase the pain. Why do I do this to myself?" I asked both her and myself.

"Let's come up with an affirmation," she suggested. "How about 'The sooner I give birth, the sooner I can see and hold my baby?'"

"Right now I don't really want to see the baby," I admitted, feeling guilty about it again. But once she suggested that, I thought more about the possibility of coming up with an affirmation and how it might help me. She stepped out for a few minutes, and when she came back, I said, "How about 'The sooner I give birth, the sooner I'll start to feel better and heal?'"

"You've had a really tough time being pregnant, haven't you?" she asked.

"Yes," I said. "I thought I'd be glowing and happier than ever. But it wasn't like that at all."

She told me that lots of women have trouble during pregnancies.

"When is the midwife coming back?" I asked.

"When she's through with the woman giving birth," she said. She explained that we'd start the suppositories all over again from the beginning because the medication has a half-life of thirty minutes. It goes away so quickly that we'd need to let it build up momentum again. At 3:40 A.M. the nurse had to leave to see another patient, and I finally drifted off to sleep.

Twice I woke feeling crampy, but I fell back asleep. Then at 5:17 A.M. I woke abruptly as my water gushed out. I started to feel some contractions, and over the next few hours they got more intense. I waited for them to come closer together and fall into a regular rhythm. They hurt, but they weren't excruciating. I had to concentrate on each one so much that I couldn't communicate during them. It was impossible to time them, as they weren't at all regular. I didn't scream. I worried about when I would feel the true pain. I concentrated on what I was doing. I didn't talk much, but I waited for the time when I'd accuse Craig of doing this to me. I wasn't yet begging for an epidural, but I figured I'd know that time when it came.

And then at 8:45 A.M. I turned to Craig and said, "I just pushed for three contractions in a row. Go get the nurse." Craig thought something was really wrong because I shouldn't be pushing only three and a half hours after my water broke and labor started. It was so early in the process that nobody had checked to see how far dilated I was, or how the baby's heart was beating, or anything. But sure enough, it was our time. The baby had started coming down, and I had started pushing that baby out.

The midwife came running in at the last minute, saying that we were the surprise of the month. At 9:12 A.M. our son was born. I gave birth standing up, which was what felt most comfortable to me. After the midwife helped with the head, Craig caught our baby as he shot into his arms like a slippery seal being thrust out. Immediately I loved him.

For the next few days, all I could say was, "I had a baby! It came out of me!" To my great surprise I realized that other than the induction medicine, we'd avoided medications and I'd given birth naturally.

The snake's gift to me was not offering me a wish or granting me the easy birth. In retrospect, the snake's gift to me was the healing effect of a positive birth experience that transformed me completely. I didn't forget the great unpleasantness of pregnancy or the pain of childbirth, but it changed into something worthwhile—not because of the baby but because the birth itself was so empowering. I had risen to the challenge. I was healed when I had no idea I'd begun a magickal working for healing.

COMMUNITY: HONOR, RESPECT, AND GRATITUDE

COMMUNITY IS THE HEART OF THIS BOOK. Each contributor here has been touched by our community in special ways—ways that are reflected in their stories. From the power of love to help us heal to rediscovering unity and our own place of power, community is the womb in which magick truly grows.

COMMUNITY/UNITY

CINNAMON MOON

This activity is something I use to encourage community harmony; it is a way of enjoying and internalizing that energy as it spirals. Begin by preparing a mixture of equal parts of the following ingredients (preferably dried, when available):

- Alfalfa—to aid material subsistence and protection
- Borage—to lend courage, bring inner joy and radiance, and neutralize difficult issues
- Cedar—to purify
- Cinnamon—to bring good fortune, purification, and communication
- Dill—to strengthen mental processes and protect
- Garlic—to strengthen and bind
- Juniper berries—to banish negative energy and entities
- Lavender—to bring peace of mind and clear thinking, and to attract material success
- Lily of the valley—to promote common sense and strengthen the mind
- Narcissus—to stimulate creativity and inspiration
- Valerian—to bring relaxation, calmness, and love

Next, gather around a central location and chant the following while you sprinkle the blend over charcoal, a fire pit, or the community brazier:

As we weave and spin our spell,
threefold return the tale will tell.
Bathe thyself in the Golden Light,
and soon all will be put right.

Continue until your voices naturally rise, creating a cone of power, and fall to a whisper again. At this point the leader of the group can close the rite with something simple, like:

Heart to heart, spirit to spirit,
with love and blessings, so mote it be!

DECENCY: A TRUE STORY OF GOODNESS AND THE POWER OF LOVE

Precious Nielsen

In early 1999 I had managed to lose myself in almost every sense of the word. I had been tricked out of the custody of my children, lost my ranch, and lost my job. Every time I found a job, a voice from the past would call my employers and tell them foul lies to make them think it was too risky to have me as an employee. The local deputies warned me that, based on their own experiences, this person was not going to stop until I either died or left the area.

After a physical attack, I felt I had to leave Texas with as much as I could move. Selling everything of any value so that I could survive until I could get a job in a location where no one was trying to cause me harm, I took off for West Virginia, only to find more disillusionment. Grief washed over me in waves.

I worked two jobs, slept little, lived in a women's shelter and out of my truck. I had no family to call for help and felt like I was one of the loneliest women on the Earth. After six weeks I'd saved enough for a new place and eventually found a space to set up some type of life again.

In July our new students came. They were all graduate students doing their internships. One woman (we'll call her Lady B) was about the same age as I, and as it turned out she remembered me from the weeks when I'd hoped to find a roommate. Lady B and I got along fabulously, despite the fact that I really didn't want to make any friends, never socialized, and was so locked in my pain that I didn't want to think of my personal life at all. Healing wasn't even an option for me at that time. I liked Lady B, though, and I knew we had a similar spiritual background. She is Wiccan and I am a shaman—albeit at that time a mere shell of the one I had been.

One day Lady B came in with a brochure for a gathering that was going to be held in Virginia and invited me to go. I asked what the fee was, knowing that if there was any fee at all I couldn't afford to go. Interestingly enough, the brochure even pictured someone I'd known thirty years before! That drove my desire to go, but I really couldn't afford it. Lady B told me she'd spring for my fee.

That was, for me, the first step in coming back. Somehow, that clever lady had trapped me into not hiding in my apartment for three entire days and had gotten me to commit to going not just out of my hole but camping with a lot of other people. We went, camped in the excitement of Tropical Storm Dennis, and had a wonderful time. I have to admit that it was pretty intense for me, and I wasn't exactly open to meeting many people there. Just being "in public," out from under my rock, camping with the wonderful energies of life around me, and experiencing the torrents of rain and the strong wind while in the company of the remarkable Lady B tugged at my soul and dragged me out of the stark darkness of my grief and pain and base level of living merely to survive that had become my only safety.

Mind you, there was still a part of me that wanted to die, but Lady B was determined that I would rejoin the living. She made sure I always had food and toilet paper—which became our joke, so she would always show up with toilet paper. She knew that sometimes when I had no money I would leave work late and take a roll of toilet paper home with me. She couldn't stand to see anyone so desperate that they would steal toilet paper. I probably owe her thirty rolls of it. And with each delivery, we talked—talked a lot. Retreat was not an option.

Sometimes I would go into denial and simply block any further movement into the world of the living. Lady B would slam the truth in my face and then get off the phone so that I had to face it without anyone willing to listen to my excuses or good reasons for denial. Throughout this time I could feel remnants of my self and my power surfacing. Sometimes I would cry with joy, and sometimes I would venture to take another baby step back toward the person I had always been.

Lady B frequently tried to get me to allow a living plant into my apartment, but I still wasn't quite that willing to let life in. I was too afraid that it, like other things I've loved, would leave me, and the pain would just be too much. I was satisfied grooming her African violet, and when she saw me give it some attention she suddenly feigned being a complete idiot about African violets. Then one day when I was at the market, I spotted a terribly sad-looking little plant. I *heard* it, in fact, and when I looked over there it was, half out of its pot with wilted leaves and some broken stems. I asked the manager if he would mark it down for me, and he did. The first living thing in my apartment had gotten in the door.

In the spring of 2000, Lady B made her move. I was once again pretty much myself, though not quite. I was no longer shunning my spirituality like a dead body. I could even speak to my children without breaking down into racking sobs. It was time for Lady B to bring out her big guns. I had two live plants in my pretty little apartment, and I was satisfied with that. I was definitely in the stage of denial at which I would deny that I was still in denial.

One day during a pouring rain, when I was innocently at work, I got a call from my dear friend. She had a favor to ask of me. She had a lot of feral cats around her house and knew that I love all animals, with a special kinship with cats and birds. She had just been outside and found one of them that was less than a year old, in a ditch, in the pouring rain, giving birth. She wanted to know if it could stay at my house. I immediately said, "No. I can't have animals." She said she would buy the food and cat litter and give me food bowls, but if she had to take the cat to the shelter, the entire lot of them would be put to sleep.

I had been successfully baited. I relented and said the cat could come, but only until she found another home for it later. Yep, there was the hook!

The cat wasn't very nice to me and scared me as best she could. I just called her Mama, since that is what she was. She was snarling when Lady B carried her up the stairs in a cat carrier and continued to snarl while she finished giving birth to a total of seven kittens. In fact, she snarled at me when I opened the door to her room to feed her or to make sure she had water, and she wouldn't eat until I left. All that cat did was snarl—and it was not a timid snarl. I knew just how she felt. Poor Mama had had no home, had given birth in the rain under the threat of death, and wasn't mean at all; she was utterly terrified.

I made it my mission to let that cat know love, but she was no more cooperative than I had been with Lady B. I'd take her food and she'd snarl. I'd talk to her soothingly and she'd snarl. I'd look at her and she'd snarl. But she didn't attack.

One day I swallowed my fears of being clawed and bitten and lay down on the floor next to the closet where Mama was nursing her kittens. She was not impressed. The snarling and yowling were ferocious! I stayed for about three minutes and then left, and she snarled for a good five minutes after I was gone. Every day I added time to my visits, and she never stopped snarling. By the end of the first week I was lying half in and half out of her closet four or five times a day, always cooing to her when I talked, and gradually edging my hand closer and closer to her babies.

Then I began touching her babies, and to my surprise and pleasure she did not attack or snarl any more fiercely. For several days I got her used to me touching her kittens, and then I let my fingertips touch her belly while I was petting them as they nursed. She studied me *very* closely and continued her snarling, but didn't move. The next time I went in,

I went through my usual process of cooing, talking, and touching her kittens, and then I openly stroked her tummy.

The most marvelous thing happened when Mama realized she was being touched. Between her snarls she let out some kind of a mangled and pathetic attempt at purring! She rolled further onto her back and spoke something very close to "purrr–reooowww–purrpurrpurr– reoooww–purrpurrpurr." I wanted to laugh out loud with delight, but satisfied myself with smiling until I had left the room to call Lady B and tell her what had occurred. Then I cried, and cried and cried and cried. I realized I had been very much like Mama, and Lady B knew that and knew exactly what she was doing when she brought me that cat I did not want to let in.

After that time, the healing came quickly with strength. Mama decided she actually loved me and followed me everywhere. She still snarls at other people, but not at me and not at Lady B. She has never bitten or clawed a person. She is a love and shares that love with me. Mama and I have each other still—along with the kitten Lady B pulled out of her in the rainstorm and a kitten from her next litter. In fact, I also have Lady B's cat, who needed to be cared for when Lady B moved to Florida.

I'm not sure where I'd be if I hadn't met my friend, and if she hadn't had the decency as a human being to care about the quality of life of a woman she barely knew, the goodness to continue trying despite how hard I fought life, and the love for all things living and for me as a friend. I know she saved my life and went far beyond the stamina most of us have for honoring our vows to heal others. Of course I played a role in my healing; one always must do the work oneself.

Now that I am again in the world of the living, with my spirit intact and blossoming once again, I realize how very extraordinary Lady B is, how much she is capable of giving, and what it looks like when we walk with the Goddess. Thank you.

MAGICK AND COMMUNITY, INCARNATE AND INCARCERATED

ASHLEEN O'GAEA

As I was growing up, mistrusting the concepts of friendship and community was taught to me as a strength. I was shown that love and trust were conditional, and was expected to understand that magick was nonsense and joy an unreasonable expectation.

I have since chosen to accept different truths about the world, and, eventually, my late parents ceded enough of their fears to be cool with my being Wiccan (once they were sure it wasn't Satanism and I wouldn't be ostracized for being outspoken about it). They wouldn't have been comfortable with my prison ministry, though, for too many of their fears and prejudices were consolidated in their absolute certainty that everyone who is incarcerated should be, and is both irredeemable and incorrigible.

My personal journey to the loving, trusting, joyous experience of friendship, community, and magick makes a fair-to-middlin' tale, but this isn't my how-I-became-a-Pagan story; you've heard plenty. You've probably not heard, though, my fairly unconventional perspective on community—Neopagan community—and on prison ministry (with which you might not be very comfortable, either). To frame it, I'll skip forward to 1987, when my husband-priest, Canyondancer, and I were among the founders of the Tucson Area Wiccan-Pagan Network (TAWN).

Tucson is, I think, one of the best and easiest places in the country to be a Neopagan of any stripe. There are several demographic reasons for this: We have the University of Arizona here and Davis-Monthan Air Force Base, both of which (no matter how you feel about the military) keep our population fresh. We have quite a lot of dynamic retirement satellites, and their residents aren't fogies. We're an hour's drive from Mexico and surrounded by tribal reservations, so multiculturalism is mother's milk around these parts. All of those factors help make Tucson Pagan friendly.

There's more to it, though; community's neither automatic nor easy. For more than a decade before TAWN was founded, individual Witches, if I may be blunt, worked their butts off to educate local law enforcement and the media about Wicca. By press release and presentation, by flyer and Open U class, a few really dedicated individuals were both bold and tireless in their efforts. Years of preparation went into creating the time and place where TAWN could come to life and community could incarnate.

With its long-standing monthly potluck meetings, which we naturally call "cauldron-lucks," the annual Fall Festival and Faire (and from 2004, the Spring Spirit Day), open Sabbats and Esbats, public classes, a Moon School for kids between the ages of four and sixteen, and a quarterly newsletter (*Tapestry*), TAWN does a lot to facilitate community. Many definitions of magick are understood here, many styles of magick taught and practiced. We share our ideas about magickal systems and readily acknowledge their distinctions; and for the most part, we're charmingly unconscious of the deepest magick we do, which is being a community.

Wherever such a community thrives, it nourishes growth around it; just as significant, its own growth is nourished by surrounding influences. To the Pagan population here, we've all brought the influences of our various involvements and callings; this is some of the diversity from which Wicca draws part of its strength. And it's one example of this exchange of energies among groups, the interconnectedness Wiccans are always talking about, that I want to share with you here.

For the life of our coven, Campsight, Canyondancer and I were fully occupied with coven duties and the additional responsibility to articulate and develop the Adventure tradition of Wicca, now gaining recognition. But even before Campsight disbanded, transferring the active steward-ship of our tradition to Hearth's Gate Coven, I was called to another priestessly vocation, one that some of my colleagues find unfathomable.

I'm a founding board member and the senior corresponding priest-ess of Mother Earth Ministries-ATC, a Neopagan prison ministry based here in Tucson. Mother Earth Ministries (MEM) was created in 2000 by Lady Carol Garr and a few other local priests and priestesses; the ATC at the end of the formal name stands for Aquarian Tabernacle Church, the internationally known and respected Wiccan church with which we're affiliated. The ATC community, from its headquarters in Index, Washington, supports MEM administratively and holds the broad per-spective we sometimes need to sight along.

Prison ministry is difficult work on every plane. We've been talking about community, and it's easy to understand prison as a place for people who've opted out of community. But in its own way, prison—like many institutions—*simulates* community. As it is to some degree for most kinds of institutions (corporate, academic, and military, for example), this mimicry is based on mistrust and conditional acceptance; and magick, when the subject comes up, tends to be taken for Disney or diabolical.

I believe that magick is a natural force, like gravity, and the choice we have with regard to it is whether to work it well or poorly, responsi-bly or recklessly. (Come to think of it, that's just about how I see com-munity, too.) Energy in Wiccan ritual circles is worked cooperatively. The energy raised in correctional institutions is worked in a "power-over" context of domination. When it's not carefully channeled, it's appropri-ated to manipulation, deceit, and revenge in the service of anger, scorn, and fear. The Wiccan password of "perfect love and perfect trust" seems pretty far removed from prison culture, where *love* is spelled "ten to twenty" and *trust* is spelled "big, heavy b-a-r-s." So are we nuts, or what? What makes us think we can make a difference to these desperadoes? Back atcha: Why should we think we *can't*?

We're men and women of faith, after all, and our faith is that magick is alive, and Goddess is afoot! She changes everything she touches, as Starhawk taught us, and when she touches inmates through our work, they change too. At the very least, as Lady Garr reminds us, it's worth a try to change the worldview of inmates who will one day be released to be your or our neighbors.

For a priestess with experience of community building, prison ministry is a wonderful opportunity to share the rewards and responsibilities of community. Reward and obligation alike come from affiliation with the Pagan community here, which has changed my life—and others'—in ways that inmates' lives need changing too. Like most newcomers to Wicca, inmates want to learn magick. We teach them that building real, healthy community *is* working magick; it's the foundation and the context that give our password meaning. Spiritually, MEM's priests and priestesses create opportunities to explore perfect love and trust for men and women who've had no such experience of their own.

It's reasonable to wonder, and many people do, whether the effort of prison ministry is the best way to direct our energies, either mundane or magickal. Our answer—and here I paraphrase my colleagues as well as speaking for myself—is that our work with MEM actually benefits the wider Neopagan community. Our skills, ritual and pastoral, are honed by prison ministry. Our creativity is stimulated: you might say that working in the box helps us think outside the box! Our sensitivity is heightened; our tact and patience develop; we become more appreciative of subtle freedoms and aware of even deeper manifestations of divinity. All this blesses us with more to contribute to the rest of the Pagan community. (None of MEM's current volunteers identifies as shaman, but like true shamans, we all use our journeys to the "Otherworld" of prison ministry to benefit our home community.)

I see the Threefold Law plainly at work here. I receive from Pagan community the gift of angers and agonies reforged to glow with joy, and I return this boon to the community threefold: if you're counting, say through the Adventure tradition, through involvement with TAWN, and through my pastoral work with inmates. But three's a magickal number and we mustn't understand it only literally, so count again: confrontation of guardians (fears and prejudices, not watchtowers) is a principal business of the tradition I follow; and it follows that helping inmates address their issues brings me face-to-face with mine. The inmates to whom I am priestess rely on me to guide them from their barred yards and inner landscapes back into the world—the world of Neopagan community.

To my pastoral work with people for whom one of the worst-case scenarios has unfolded, I bring as a priestess theological understanding that the energies of misfortune can be reclaimed. For many inmates, love and trust and joy are theoretical at best; their experience is of worlds of exploitation, opportunism, betrayal, and fear. The realization alone that there is a Neopagan community founded on different values and premises, with personal experience of it still an anticipation, can work magick in their lives.

I can personally understand the pain of needing yet fearing to love yourself and trust others. I can articulate the longing for unconditional love and let the Goddess's promises of it shine through my letters to inmates. I can offer assurance that there's a magick that's neither Disney nor diabolical, and very real indeed. In advice and by example I can model acceptance and assertion of personal boundaries without anger, and learning to keep expectations of other people realistic; and I can present these skills as learnable and relevant to magick. My colleagues and I genuinely assure inmates that they matter—to us, to the God/ Goddess, and to the Neopagan communities they hope someday to join.

I liken prison ministry to journeying in the Otherworld. Through letters from inmates, I've encountered some horrors I'd rather have avoided . . . and even more joys I might otherwise have overlooked. The depths of fear and hope this work has helped me fathom, and the resilience of humanity's innate sense of wonder I've been privileged to witness, have added dimension to my life—and have thus enriched all the communities I'm part of. It's a holy mystery that the narrowness of prison walls can widen our horizons! This is one of those disguised magicks Adventure Wiccans expect to encounter "around the next bend." It's a magickal journey, the path to community, and one can—and does—start on either side of the bars.

For that matter, we're all behind bars of one sort of another. Shadow guardians, my tradition calls them: ignorance and fears and prejudices that shackle us as surely as handcuffs and leg irons. But there's room for magick in even the smallest of cells, and I'm going to share a little magick with you right now, the same way I share it with inmates: on paper.

A community vow

Here's an "incanted vow," something you can read or recite as dramatically as you like, or in a whisper if you need to. Let it hearten and sanctify your own pledge of—your offering to and your growth in—community, and your awareness of the magick it works. With blessings.

> By aspect and circumstance, in each Direction!
> By text and remembrance; indenture, release!
> Now steady, now trembling, by dread and affection,
> alone and assembling; in conflict, at peace!
> By turf and by flame, by brook and by breeze,
> by my spirit's disturbance, and by my heart's ease;
> by lock and by bar, by freedom and key,
> by moon and by star, by error and harmony:
> to he who is Horn, and she who is Three,
> to once- and re-born, to all and to me,
> by wine and by corn, I vow community!

—Ashleen O'Gaea—

NURTURING THE NURTURERS

CARL McCOLMAN

A question I've often asked is, who nurtures the nurturers? Too often I've seen, not only in the Pagan community but in other spiritual traditions as well, situations where the priests, priestesses, or other community leaders seem to give, give, give of themselves until they're burned out, exhausted, and all too often bitter and resentful. Is it any wonder? Recovery programs warn us that problems are more likely to occur when we're hungry, angry, lonely, or tired—and it seems that the spiritual nurturers I've known are, thanks to the constant demands placed on them, often among the hungriest, angriest, loneliest, and most tired of people. If we as a community don't take care of our nurturers, they won't be there to nurture us—at least, not for long.

I found an answer to my question when my own life seemed to be spiraling utterly out of control. It was the summer of 2002—and one lazy Sunday morning I drove an hour from my home to attend the local council meeting for the Covenant of the Goddess. It was an uneventful meeting, as meetings go. But while driving home, I received a frantic phone call from my wife, Fran. She was at the mall, where our teenage daughter, Rhiannon, had just vomited blood all over the restroom.

It was a phone call I had been dreading for years. Rhiannon had been born with severe polycystic kidney disease, which among many other problems caused fibrous tissue to form on her liver. As a result, there were issues with the normal flow of blood in her abdomen, leading to a variety of dangerous possibilities, including severe nosebleeds, bloody stools, and the formation of varices (varicose veins) along the wall of her esophagus. If those veins burst, vomiting blood could result—which could be fatal.

I met Fran and Rhiannon at the hospital. Rhiannon, looking pale as a ghost, sat with a confused expression on her face, as if she didn't fully comprehend the gravity of her situation. Fran and I held each other and tried to find the best way to answer the doctor's questions about advance directives, organ harvesting, and other topics that a parent hopes never to face regarding a child. Finally Rhiannon went into emergency surgery, and Fran and I tried to figure out what our lives would look like while she remained in the hospital.

The surgery went well, and although Rhiannon spent a couple of days in the intensive care unit, we were hopeful that the damage in her esophagus had been repaired—at least enough that she could go home. But within a few hours of being discharged from the ICU, she vomited more blood. This time, in the hospital, they could measure the amount: a quart of her precious life was expelled into the container.

Another emergency procedure followed, after which Rhiannon was heavily sedated and placed on a respirator in order to allow the fragile walls in her esophagus a chance to heal. Fran and I were numb. Would this nightmare scenario just replay until we lost her?

Thankfully, it didn't. Our girl remained in the ICU over a week and logged nearly two full weeks in the hospital before finally going home— and more than a dozen day surgeries over the next eighteen months, as her doctor carefully repaired the damage in her esophagus. But of course, as we held each other and Rhiannon while a quart of her blood sat on the counter, we had no way of knowing if we would be facing a miracle or the heartbreak of our lives.

Who nurtures the nurturers? Fran and I have been active in the Earth spirituality community for years, having led semipublic rituals and a bimonthly meditation group. And so the answer came to us in a variety of ways during those two weeks in July and early August 2002: *everyone* nurtures the nurturers.

The first day Rhiannon went into the emergency room, I went home to pick up clothing and other essentials—and to send out an email letting people know what had happened. That one message was all it took. Soon the phones were ringing—our cell phones and the hospital phone once Rhiannon had her own room. The flowers, balloons, and stuffed animals began to pour in—along with food and Bach flower essences for her mom and dad. Every time I checked email, more expressions of love, support, magick, prayer, and Reiki were flowing in from literally around the world.

A friend who works for public television arranged to have an entire case of videos sent to Rhiannon, free of charge. A Pagan chiropractor showed up and gave Fran and me complimentary adjustments. A Q'ero-trained (Inca) shamanic healer came into Rhiannon's room in the ICU and performed a healing ceremony, stones and feathers and all (the nurses discreetly looked the other way). Fran's meditation teacher was with us it seemed constantly, holding us, chanting with us, or silently offering his loving presence. A member of the band Three Weird Sisters showed up one afternoon with her guitar and performed for Rhiannon for almost an hour—at one point suddenly having to censor the words to "Boys Want Sex in the Morning" when a nurse wandered into the room! Visitors (both Pagan and non-Pagan) offered to sit with Rhiannon for ten minutes or three hours, to give Fran and me a chance to take a breather or go grab a meal. The emails kept pouring in, offering love and energy and, most of all, nurture. Nurture for Rhiannon—and nurture for her unspeakably grateful parents.

In Welsh myth, the goddess Rhiannon (of course) scolds her human lover when he doesn't ask for what he wants. How often do we mortals make the same mistake? And I think the nurturers are often the worst at letting others know about our wants and needs. It's humbling, of course, to be the needy one. And yet *humility* means "of the Earth." We who walk by the wisdom of the Earth need always to keep this in mind.

A year later Rhiannon, still living under the shadow of her kidney disease but nevertheless joyful and very much alive, was given a precious gift: the doctor who repaired her esophagus nominated her for the Make-a-Wish Foundation, and so she manifested her lifelong dream of visiting Walt Disney World (with her lucky mom and dad tagging along). Dazzled by Mickey and company, we were amused by the resort's motto: "Where magic lives." Sure, seeing Rhiannon glow as the Disney folks treated her like a princess was magickal enough. But we knew from those harrowing days the previous summer where magick *really* lives: in the hearts of all who love.

PAGAN CLUSTER IN CALGARY: A SHORT REPORT ON THE G8 PROTESTS

STARHAWK

[Note: The G8 conference of 2002 was a meeting among the world's most industrialized countries in order to make decisions that would have crucial global impacts, from economics to humanitarian considerations. Unfortunately, average folk wishing to have a voice in such matters were not necessarily welcomed with open arms. —Patricia Telesco]

July 3, 2002: We arrived in Calgary from multiple different directions, at different times. We came from Seattle, California, Texas, Vermont, Colorado, Kansas, British Columbia, Ottawa, Alberta, and other parts of Canada. Our first challenge was crossing the threshold, the border. All of us were challenged, questioned, searched. Some of us had to try twice or even three times. But all of us got in.

We brought with us a variety of practical and magickal skills, from the knowledge of how to design an ecological garden to the skills of organizing a street action, from knowing how to convert a diesel engine to run on veggie oil to knowing how to facilitate a meeting. We were welcomed, supported, and taken in by the wonderful Witches of Calgary, the organizers of the action, as well as by Kelly and Marie, the practicing permaculturists who opened their home to hordes of us visiting and making magick.

We arrived in a city drenched in fear and hostility, with everyone from the media to the school board portraying the protesters as dangerous, malevolent, and violent. Teachers and students were ordered not to talk to us. An "expert" lectured the judges and magistrates of the city, telling them we were coming to kill cops, among other warped fantasies. People who might have rented spaces to us were warned we would bomb them or burn down their homes.

The organizers of the action were working nonstop, trying to combat the propaganda and arrange for spaces and infrastructure in an extremely hostile environment. They welcomed us, and we tried to see what we could do to support them. As the cluster gathered, we wove our magick, trancing together, reading tarot cards to ask for guidance and information. We clarified our intention: "Our intention is to consciously use the energy and actions of this week to shift the ground beneath the fortress of power-over and undermine its foundations so that it crumbles, opening space to seed loving cultures of beauty, balance, and delight."

We were told to go on the summer solstice to the statue of the Famous Five in Olympic Plaza. The Five were the women who brought a court case that established that women in Canada were legally persons. They stand around an inscribed circle that was just big enough for the group that gathered. We created a magickal drain, a vortex to suck away the fear that clouded the city, and a positive pole, a tree of life to draw in positive forces.

Over the next two nights, we communicated in trance with the Reclaiming Clanhouse (home base) to build our magickal group mind, and decided to use the proximity of the G8 summit as an opportunity to enter the fortress of power-over itself. We could enter the fortress, we found, through the fortress within, because each of us has a fortress inside of us. The path we took started as a passage through the clan-house. Many of our friends around the world joined us in this working, as did a number of the action organizers and the legal team. We found the fortress full of prisoners who needed to be released before we could bring it down. A green haze, green twining vines, and tunneling rabbits and prairie dogs were some of our allies in bringing it down, but mostly we understood that it will fall when the ground beneath it shifts and the spell of compliance that knits its stones and concrete together is broken.

Throughout all the following days, various members of the gathering were offering permaculture workshops, direct action training sessions, and training for the labor unions; making art and props; attending spokescouncil meetings; doing uncounted interviews with the media; and generally carrying out all the usual organizing activities associated with an action.

The next day, the actions began with a permitted family march sponsored by the unions. The Pagan Cluster participated, but we felt somewhat scattered. Some of us were part of the Bread and Puppets pageant; others were simply walking and marching.

On the full moon, the Witches of Edmonton led us in a ritual with support from the Calgary Witches, who found a beautiful, safe space with a full Chartres-style labyrinth. Many, many people from the action attended. Out of the labyrinth, a chant emerged:

We are the rising of the moon,
We are the shifting of the ground.
We are the seed that takes root,
When we bring the fortress down.

We released our fears and grief, charged moonstones and seed balls made in permaculture workshops, and danced the spiral under the full moon.

The day after, we marched off and did an impromptu spiral dance back at the Famous Five statue. By the evening, during the Showdown at the Hoedown—an unpermitted march to protest the huge party the city of Calgary was throwing for press and delegates to the G8—we had better Pagan Cluster banners and were able to march together and start a spontaneous and very powerful spiral dance outside the stadium grounds at the end. After the circle was opened, a young man was heard to exclaim, "What was that?"

We rose very early the next morning to participate in the snake march, the most confrontational action of the day, which moved through the streets of downtown Calgary during rush hour with the goal of creating economic disruption. As people gathered, the Cluster led a spiral dance. The march was peaceful: the police simply stood back, blocked traffic ahead of us, and let us take the space. People on the march made an effort to apologize to drivers, distribute leaflets, and engage in open discussion with passersby. The unions supported the march, and turned out with their flags and banners. The Cluster planted the seed balls and led another spiral at City Hall. At 10:00 A.M., after hours of marching, we all stopped and split the demonstrators into green and red groups—green to do leafleting or go on to the planned die-in, red to continue with confrontational actions. We were asked by the Anti-Capitalist Convergence if we would come on the "red" march as support for their plan to block intersections with anarchist soccer. Those of us who still had some energy had short careers either as players, rooters, or anarchist soccer moms; but we were eventually all exhausted after hours of marching in the hot sun and went on to the memorial for Carlos Giuliani (a G8 protester killed in Genoa), performed by Bread and Puppets, and the die-in. Then we went to a picnic organized by the Labour Council and Council of Canadians, where the Calgary Witches had created a beautiful healing space, with massage (definitely needed by then!), Reiki, and food and water.

Afterward, a contingent of the Cluster joined a caravan of more than a hundred cars that drove out to Kananaskis, where the G8 delegates were meeting, and after some tense negotiations (and a lengthy meeting that was, depending on your take, either an empowering impromptu blockade or a disempowering, painfully long meeting) we had yet another spiral dance, the third cone of the day.

On Thursday, we had organized our own ritual action, Earth People, which began with a circle near our favorite Famous Five statue. After casting a circle and calling directions, about sixty people covered them-

selves with mud, abandoning their powers of speech and normal
locomotion. The following prophecy was read:

When eight kings in a fortress meet
Trading greed and lies
Out of asphalt and concrete
Beings of earth arise

Grunting, dancing through the street
Ancient powers awake
In everyone they touch or meet
Hidden chains now break

The kings trade lies and costly gifts
Protected by their walls
But when the ground beneath them shifts
The mighty fortress falls

Fertile compost out of blight
Living seeds take root
Of beauty, balance and delight
Trees bear living fruit

No army can keep back a thought
No fence can chain the sea
The earth cannot be sold or bought
All life shall be free!

The army of Earth People stalked, danced, and slithered through downtown Calgary, followed by winged Beings of Liberation and beautiful
banners proclaiming "Resist!" and "Insurrection!" Alarming and delight-
ing the public, they stopped at the Gap and at the headquarters of major
oil companies to perform a dance ritual of awakening, rising, uprooting
the anchors of corporate power, and planting seeds. Drumming and chanting
built the energy to a peak again and again, and the Earth People succeeded in completely taking the streets. Mesmerized members of the
public followed, and the action became an impromptu snake march,
with amazing energy. It ended at Eau Claire Market shopping center

with a spiral dance, and then a procession down to the river and a ritual bathing. At the moment the circle was opened, raindrops fell and thunder and lightning filled the sky.

After returning to what passes for our normal state of consciousness, eating, and showering, we went back to the convergence center for the debriefing and led a closing circle and spiral dance.

The last night, after a final permaculture workshop for about twenty people and a last set of media interviews, we went back to the fortress in trance with much of the Cluster and many of the organizers. The trance was long and complex, and maybe we'll try to write up the notes later; but the essence was that the fortress is huge, with many chambers and aspects, but we have begun shifting some of its energies. One yearling bear was killed up at Kananaskis by the military this week, and the bear's spirit came with us as an ally. We tried to go up the stairs into the higher levels of the fortress, but found ourselves drifting in confusion and decided the time was not yet right. We found a crack in the walls that let us enter the structure of the fortress itself. We entered a tunnel that was very old and existed in multiple times, especially the Roman Empire. In one chamber, we were stirring a cauldron of black stuff, like oil or like the dark lava flowing under the earth, until the vortex became a spindle revolving. The ancestors from the Burning Times were with us. And then many of us took hands, jumped into the cauldron, and fell through into another world in which we were birds circling around the towers of the fortress, weaving a cocoon of binding and transformation.

We're thinking that in the next action we might need to work with Air. We've held the energy of Water, of the living river, since the Quebec protests. In January, at the World Economic Forum, we brought in Brigid's flame and the energy of Fire. In this action, we held Earth. So Air seems to be next.

The actions were small this time, never more than five thousand people, but for Calgary, everyone says, they were big. And a major international mobilization was never called for Calgary—in fact, there was a conscious call put out for people to focus on their home communities instead of using huge resources to converge on the summit there. Some very positive things came out of the actions. Ties and connections with the labor movement (at least in Canada) were strengthened, and the unions gained valuable experience in direct action that they may put to use in their own struggles. The global justice movement in Calgary was strengthened, and organizers here will have a stronger base to build on. The actions were extremely peaceful; in fact, some of us would have liked more of an edge of confrontation (which is not at all the same thing as violence). However, the utter politeness and calm of the protests may have done more than anything else could have to delegitimize the G8 and point out the obscenity of its militarization and the $300 million it spent on security.

As for the Pagan Cluster, we were able to deepen our magick, our ability to create a magickal group mind, to share our work openly with the whole action in a transparent way, and to create an action of our own that turned out to be one of the most exciting moments of the week.

Many thanks to all in the community who participated and who gave us such great support—especially to Tarra, who found housing for many of us, found the space for the full moon ritual, and did countless other acts of organizing and kindness; to the Edmonton Witches who created the Full Moon ritual; to Kelly and Marie, who let their home be taken over for weeks, helped organize, plan, and teach the permaculture workshops, and supported us in our border trials and everything else; to the organizers and legal collective who helped us with everything from immigration to traffic tickets; and to all who gave us magickal, practical, financial, and moral support.

STONE SOUP CASSEROLE

LAURA PERRY

This casserole was inspired by the often-told children's story "Stone Soup," in which a whole community comes together to create a delicious pot of soup when supposedly there was no food to be had. I invented this dish for a Goddess 2000 Project event that featured a food drive for the Atlanta Community Food Bank as well as a potluck dinner for the event participants. The casserole includes the ingredients that the story's villagers added to a traveler's "stone soup"—cabbage, salt beef, potatoes, carrots, and onions.

To make it a truly "Stone Soup" dish, have each person bring one ingredient and then combine them together as a community. *Do not* use a stone as one of the ingredients. Yes, that would be in keeping with the story, and stones are often used as sacred items in the Pagan community; but heating a stone to the temperature required to cook this casserole will likely make it explode, and that certainly won't add to the energy of the dish (or your oven).

Note that the story "Stone Soup" includes salt beef as one of the ingredients in the soup; hence the dried beef in my casserole recipe.

For a vegetarian dish, either substitute soy bacon or simply leave out this ingredient. The casserole will still be delicious.

8 ounces wide egg noodles
¼ head of green cabbage, shredded
1 cup dried beef, finely chopped
3 russet potatoes, peeled and diced
2 carrots, peeled and diced
1 yellow onion, chopped
1 can condensed French onion soup
1 can condensed cream of celery soup
  Breadcrumbs or crushed crackers (optional)

Preheat the oven to 350°F. Cook the noodles in boiling salted water until just tender. Drain them well and place in a buttered 9 by 13-inch casserole dish or baking pan. Add the cabbage, dried beef, potatoes, carrots, onion, and both soups, and mix well. If you like, top the casserole with breadcrumbs or crushed crackers. Cover tightly with aluminum foil and bake for 40 minutes, or until the vegetables are tender (check a hunk of potato with a fork to be sure). Uncover and bake another 10 minutes, or until the top is nicely browned. Share with your friends. Serves 4 to 6.

TOUCHING THE COMMUNITY, AND THE COMMUNITY TOUCHING ME

ARDY

How has the community touched my life? I need to narrow that question so it's more local. How has the PhoenixPhyre Phamily (of Florida) touched my life? Are these the same thing? No, not really. There is a greater Pagan community than the PhoenixPhyre Phamily, but I'm not as actively involved with it. Even so, I am treated as a respected crone in both the Florida Phamily and the greater community. And how I am treated has touched my life; it has made me more aware of how I treat the Phamily and the greater community. I could, perhaps, be the queen bitch crone of Florida—I have the potential for it—but not many folks would be willing to put up with that attitude for very long.

I find myself thinking in terms of community nowadays, more than in terms of just my circle family. And that mind-set seems to be the function of elders of many cultures, to think in terms of the whole community: men, women, children, every age. When we were putting together our ritual for 2004, I constantly had to remind some of the facilitators that we were leading the ritual for the whole Phamily: it was not about just the crones. I was surprised some of them did not seem to understand that basic truth, and that understanding is necessary when you are dealing with a large mixed bag of people.

I know if I say to the larger Pagan community that I see something harmful happening, they will listen to me. That knowledge makes me take more care in thinking about what I say to the community at large before I say it. It's strange, isn't it? When you know you can move a whole community, you have to be more careful, and perhaps a bit more compassionate in your statements. This is how community, both in the local and in the broader sense, has touched me and affected me every day.

community and communication

For one whole week, listen to your words, especially when you're around other members of the community. How do your words affect others? How do they affect you and your aura? Tape-record some conversations and think about how positive or negative you're being, then make viable efforts to remain aware of the changes you need to make. Transform your words, and you transform your interactions. You also transform your thoughts, for that is where action begins.

—Patricia Telesco—

YULETIDE

MIKE SHORT

Many years ago, when I was a younger, lighter man with a spring in my step and color in my beard, I was invited to play Santa at the community center in Reston, Virginia. This was before I began to follow a Celtic Wiccan, Pagan path, but also well after I had become estranged from my upbringing as a Lutheran.

I had a costume made that fitted me well (since it was handmade and designed—intentionally—to make me look fatter) and was not quite the American Santa seen in most magazine advertisements. I'd had some experience in the use of stage makeup, and with help from my female friends, I developed a makeup that weathered my face and turned my hair, beard, and eyebrows white.

In the first year I found that I could listen to the kids who came to see me and, by repeating what they asked for, let their parents know exactly what they wanted for Christmas. I also found that it was wise to have a good supply of candy canes to hand out to the kids. It let me give them something immediately to reinforce my assurance that they were good kids. (I'm not sure, however, that I was doing their parents any favors: sugaring up the excited tykes just before they went home was probably unkind at best.) It was really easy to be Santa if I just took the time to relax before going in and to embrace a mental image of who and what Santa was.

Then in the second year, something odd began to happen. The local Jewish kids began to come to me to tell me about what they wanted for Hanukkah. The kids of Asian ancestry began to come to me too, excited by the season but telling me about their own customs (nominally Christian), which their parents had brought with then from Korea or Thailand or Japan. Santa wasn't fazed by this; he listened, learned, and talked and laughed a lot!

And then I noticed that some of the kids were coming to talk to me about problems they had in their young lives. School grades featured largely, of course, but also sick family or friends, feeling bad about their own behavior or the behavior of friends, and other things that loomed large in their lives. Oddly, I never seemed to have a problem listening, and most of the time found I had comments to make. Sometimes I swear I was pulling things to say out of my . . . hat. But it worked! The kids all (or at least mostly) left happy.

It was in the third year that I began to think that there was something else going on here. The company where I was working for my regular job was thinking about putting on cleaning staff, which under ordinary circumstances wouldn't affect me, but the human resources guy had been by my office on a Friday to ask if I had anyone I could send over. I took his card, stuck it in my pocket, and told him I'd ask around, but since I was going to be busy as Santa over the weekend I didn't think I'd have any luck.

Then on Sunday, I'd been talking with kids and completely lost track of time. It was a real surprise when the staff told me that they needed to close now. It was late and dark already, so I decided I'd just duck out the back door and drive my truck home in costume. I stuffed my civvies into my big red bag, slung it over my shoulder, grabbed a couple of candy canes to give to my own kids, and hit the back door.

I was trotting around the end of the building and out toward the parking lot (still in Santa mode) when I noticed a man and a woman with two small kids standing under the streetlamp at the public phone. Their (old) car was pulled up to the curb next to the phone. I had to go right past them to reach my truck. So I just ran over and chatted up the kids, giving them each a candy cane. They were tired and frightened, but Santa got them smiling and relaxed. Then I turned to their parents and asked what was up.

The father had just packed up his family and traveled to Reston to take a job as a custodian. The job, however, had evaporated while they were driving up from one of the Carolinas. The guy that he'd spoken to was going to spring for a hotel night, but then they'd be out of luck, with no job either here or back home. Then he asked me if I knew of a cheap hotel. As it happens, I was aware of one nearby, so I gave him directions.

Then he asked me if I knew of any jobs. I reached into my shirt pocket (which happened to be on top of the stuff in my bag), pulled out the human resources guy's card, and gave it to the fellow, saying he should go there tomorrow morning and say that Santa had sent him for a job. Then I ran back around the building and waited for them to leave before I got into my truck to drive home.

On Monday I got in very early and called my human resources contact. By coincidence (yeah, right) the man was already in, getting ready to place a newspaper ad for the jobs he wanted to fill. I told him the story and primed him to play straight man when or if the father from Carolina came looking for a job. He did, and he did well on the interview. Santa was written in as a reference, with absolutely no twitch on the part of my human resources buddy. The new guy worked there for almost seven months before he figured out where he knew me from (he let me live).

Now if you've read this far into this article, you may wonder why I've written it, and what it's doing in this book. That's easy: in retrospect, this incident was the turning point in my life. I have always enjoyed helping people, but there was a dimension to my Santa experiences that got my attention. The combination of knowing how to answer every question from both the kids in the community center and the family in the parking lot finally got me thinking. It was really too much to have had a job open at work, meet someone who needed a job and wanted to do that kind of work, and just happen to have the means of bringing them together. And of course, there was the part about making it look like Santa had just reached into his big red bag to grab a card!

Knowing what I do now, the fact that I was drawing down the Lord in the aspect of Santa seems oddly natural. In fact, these days I do it regularly—he's my personal power base. I wear red and white when I do magickal work, unless I'm skyclad. (No wisecracks, please, about my *still* being all red and white.) I've grown physically to resemble the "old elf." My hair and beard are white, I have laugh lines around my eyes, and I absolutely need my little round reading glasses just to get by. Way too many people, kids and adults these days, take it for granted that I can and will listen to their hopes and dreams—not just for Yule, but all year 'round. That is part of being active in a community.

Santa, Father Christmas, the Yule-tompta, the Winter King, and others—even St. Nicholas—and I seem to have merged. My view of life has changed because of his entry into my life—and I will not change it, even if I could.

RITUALS FOR LIFE

L IFE ITSELF IS A RITUAL. If you think about it, humans are creatures of habit. We go to work the same way daily; we use the same coffee cup. As magickal beings, however, part of our job is to take that routine and integrate our spirituality into it so we become our own gurus, guides, priests, or priestesses. The stories that follow are about that journey to awakening—about our rituals for life.

BURDEN BASKET

Jesse Wolf Hardin

*The farther you get in the nearer you come to its
essence. When you come to the One that gathers all
things up into itself, there you must stay.*

—Meister Eckehart—

Kokopelli! Kokopelli! His is a most melodic name. It rolls off the
tip of the tongue like a child exiting a slide, its consonants forming
notes that rise and fall like the laughter of rivers. Go ahead—say it
aloud: *Ko-ko-pel-lee.* He comes from the South, the direction of intimacy
and trust, and among the many gifts he brings is a particular lesson . . .
especially for us.

His is the figure of the hunchbacked flute player carved on the pink
and purple cliffs of Southwestern mesa and canyonland, from Casas
Grandes in Mexico to the San Juan basin, from the California desert to
the pueblos of the Rio Grande. Petroglyphs (carved into the dark surface
patina of stone to expose the lighter rock below) and pictographs (daubed
on with a brush of pounded plant fiber soaked in earthen pigment)
of Kokopelli date back at least to 200 C.E. recording his influence on

far-flung cultures over a long period of time. He's most often found
with what appears to be a horn or antlike antennae, a hunched back, a
flute in hand, and knees in the air as if dancing—a Pied Piper of things
wild and free, ecstatic and unruly. More often than not he'll be seen to
have an enlarged phallus, attesting to his role as seed bearer and fertility
god, the guarantor of new crops in the spring, new life in the bellies of
village women.

Many of the petroglyph spreads I've seen place Kokopelli in the
company of a plumed snake. According to my Mayan friends, the original
Kokopellis were emissaries of the feathered serpent god Quetzalcoatl,
whose return is prophesied to coincide with a period of global transformation. They carried gifts with them from the elders of the Maya of
southern Mexico and Guatemala to the northern peoples (the Anasazi
and Mogollon peoples, later known as the Hopi and Pueblo). These gifts
are said to include the four sacred colors of which Black Elk spoke
some four centuries later, pottery-making techniques, and the seeds to
grow corn. These ancient emissaries are said to have been vested with
many of the qualities of a god and the skills of a sorcerer, including the
powers to predict, to heal, and to ensure fertility among all those they
blessed with a visit.

At the Hopi village of Oraibi, Kokopelli is said to carry a bag full of
deerskin shirts to trade for wives. Other Hopi stories tell of his wife,
Kokopelli-mana, exciting the villagers into a night of passionate sex with
the teasing gestures of her dance. Whenever we find Kokopelli-mana
carved on the cliffs, she's positioned directly behind her mate, holding
his back as if she were attached, supporting his every act. At San Ildefonso
Pueblo, Kokopelli is known as a wandering minstrel with a sack of
music on his back, trading new songs for old ones. Listen to these stories.
Burnished on lava-burned boulders long before gene-damaging nuclear
tests and radioactive waste, toxic chemicals and deadly street drugs, the
hump on Kokopelli is obviously no hunched back, no deformity. It is,
rather, his burden basket.

*As I walk through the winter forest, the courage that I sense is
a quiet courage, not the courage for great heroic deeds, but for
humility to live with loss. We need such courage to face those
losses and see in them the source of new visions: a courage to
nourish the seed beneath the snow.*

—Fred Taylor—

Both physical and metaphorical, the burden basket is yet another shared
concept common to a wide range of primal cultures. The basket may
contain nothing but the personal quandaries or seemingly overwhelming
responsibilities of an individual's life, or it may be filled all the way to
the top, brimming with the joy, needs, and anguish of an entire planet as
experienced by each sensitized bearer. Its freight is a product of our
emotional engagement and the degree of sensory input we allow access
to our psyches. The more conscious, alert, and caring the person, the
heavier the load. The more we allow the eyes to see, the ears to hear,
and the heart to feel, the more we pack into the basket.

Enter the cooing of babies, the weight of parental relationship, the
redeeming reality of familial love. A lifetime of lessons. Accomplishment.
Dreams of the night and visions of the day. The experience of and desire
for smells and sights, new sounds and a familiar touch. The passion
for fruit. The coming and going of lovers, and the lessons each leaves
behind. People and places and ideas we become attached to, stored
carefully where we can find them. Kisses and art next to laughter and
sighs, retrievable memories at the top, with precious hope lying deepest
in the basket.

But do leave room for disappointment and the strength it engenders.
For personal failure and the humility that comes with it. For the certainty of bodily death, the frustration of failed campaigns to save the life
of the planet, the silent screams of humanity's unrealized dreams. Enter
the dulled and practiced laughs of those pretending to be happy while
a persistent emptiness eats at their guts. Enter the unwanted children
you see propping up lampposts on your way to work. Add the prayers of
the battered wife, the suicidal husband, the hopeful actress who never
really gets to live the roles she has no hand in writing. Add the taste of

chemicals in the water. The taste of defeat. The scent of lost lovers. The noxious odor of fumes emanating from the foundry, the refinery, the smelter, the paper mill, the megalithic sewage plant, the tar truck, the congested freeway, and the garbage cans lined up like silent tin soldiers on the street.

Then if we add conscious identification with the nonhuman world, the basket strains at the seams, stuffed with the flight of birds and the celebrations of indomitable coyotes, the desires of elk in fall, the contentment of shellfish, the anxious calling of the salmon. Followed for balance and truth by mountains groaning at the attacks of strip mines, Earth pierced by fence posts and oil wells, leveled for golf courses and condominiums. Pack it with the majority of rivers, dying behind dams. With creatures big and small, shot, trapped, and poisoned, crushed by unfeeling cars and trucks, denied more and more habitat until faced with the complete and irreversible extinction of their kind. For the truly sensitive, for the conscious and awakened examples of humanity making use of every unhampered sense, every vital instinct, it can be one heavy basket. Those who see and feel enough, those given to love, truly can be said to carry the weight of the world—on willing shoulders.

The key word here is *willing.* One usually has the option of keeping it light, of ignoring the gravity of unfolding events while suppressing intuition, instinct, and emotion. In modern society, illusions receive widespread support and denial is seen as an acceptable way of coping. On the other hand, for the most conscious and engaged, the basket may house the accumulated transgressions of our kind, the mistakes of the past, and the formidable weight of our future choices. Yet always it's a load we voluntarily pick up and carry. Unlike the powerful metaphor of the cross, no authority figure assigns the burden of the basket, no vested human judge sentences us to carry ponderous awareness through the streets of a new Jerusalem. For Kokopelli, the flowers are as important as the crown of thorns they fell from. They're to be worn not on the forehead but as pointed messages of awakeness on those prickly bushes that line the trails of our mortal lives.

The basket also differs from the cross by being a testament to aware, voluntary participation rather than blind obedience. But both speak of the essential ingredient, devotion. For Kokopelli, for the non-human world, and for primal humanity, that devotion is to sacred life, to flesh and God in unbroken unity—sensory, emotional, and spiritual interaction with the rest of the Earth-body in a glad and holy communion. The lifting of the basket is a matter of tuning in to the ecstasy as well as the agony of uninsulated, unmitigated perception. It is willing participation in destiny, the response-ability inherent in consciousness, and the acceptable consequences of our acts of love.

The nice thing about the basket is that you can always put it down when you need to. Nobody is watching, and besides, you were the one who put it on in the first place. You're trying to do everything on your list; but who wrote the list, after all? Lay down the cross for even a minute and the Roman centurions, the dream police, the eye in the sky will see to your immediate punishment. The burden basket is a different story altogether. Set it down, and be assured you will be the first to know when you've rested enough and when the time has come to move ahead with it again. There's no way to post a basket in the ground, or to nail you to it. When you're not moving, in simply lies in full view in the corner. When it is really felt is when you move with it, carrying out the course of action it inspired in you, instigating through you the necessary cures to the specific malaise. The basket is a mixed blessing, containing both the high price and the ultimate reward for your willingness to feel—your willingness to share a living world's pleasure and pain, your inspiration to respond actively and accordingly.

Wherever the image of Kokopelli is found, with bent, laden back and flute in hand—cast into silver earrings, misappropriated for trendy café menus, or carved into crimson canyon rock—a single message cries out: no matter how heavy the load, we must all dance our dance, live our song.

To fail to join in is often to fail to enjoy. Interestingly enough, those who eschew the burden of the basket are the least likely to dance, the least likely to fly. But for the load bearers every movement is a dance, as they make their way gracefully and powerfully through the obstacles and pitfalls, delights and desires of their destined paths. For the basket wearer, every utterance is a sincere demonstration, every shout both an urgent warning and an exclamation of gladness—glee that reverberates off looming high-rises as it does off the rising Anasazi cliffs.

As I write this in my Southwestern canyon home, we mindfully set a match to the wood in the fire circle, practicing the vulnerable widening of perception, opening up our individual baskets to the instructive world around us. Tonight is a night of power, and we remain vigilant for the arrival of new experience, new revelation, new depths of compassion to pack in with all the rest. Off to the side of us, just beyond the reach of firelight, we feel a certain power entertaining the darkness. Somehow, from his place of concealment, he's able to excite our physical and spiritual engagement, able to encourage the intensity of our assigned quests. It is the spirit of Kokopelli, providing us with a magickal, visual metaphor: setting the example of a basket so heavy—and a heart so big.

opening your Burden Basket

Kokopelli reminds us of the conscious choices we make in what we accept for our burden basket What burdens do you willingly carry? What ones should you put down so that you have space for new experiences, new memories, new receiving and giving?

See what's inside yours, how much of it is really useful, helpful, motivational—and how much comes from unrealistic expectations of the sacred self. Choose what you place in that basket, and know when your life's ritual calls on you to carry it, or put it down and simply be. Record your thoughts in your spiritual diary.

—Patricia Telesco—

DANCE FROM
YOUR BELLY

LOBA

Once upon a time I did not know my home, my purpose, my soul mate, my river . . . I lived on the dark sides of cities among strangers speaking a language I did not understand. I lived in a search for substance and meaning, for love and a sense of belonging. I remember all too well the uneasy feeling of walking the city streets, so disconnected from the Earth that I was like a balloon somebody had let go, a thin string dangling, reaching helplessly toward the ground from way up in the drifting clouds. I remember my *butoh* dance mentor commending me on my energy, my passion; but, she said, "You are too much out here" (waving her arms around). "You need to dance from your belly!"

I tried desperately to heed her advice, but how could I dance from my belly when I was in denial about having one? I shaved my head every week for more than a year. What was it I was trying to shed? I didn't even know, I just knew I had to continue the purging ritual till that something was gone. On the Night of the Dead in San Francisco, I painted my whole body black, with splashes of red lipstick that looked like blood, and danced like a maniac through the streets till I fell back intentionally, my skull hitting the pavement. My performance artist friends danced all around me—trying to raise me from the dead, I suppose. I just wanted them to leave me alone as I came to the realization: I had never in my life built a fire. I had never built a fire.

Finally I got out of the city for a week, my first extended visit to the wilds in years: I was with my crew of crazy friends, and out there on the wild Lost Coast I felt I loved them more than I ever had before. But when it was time to go back to the city, all of a sudden I just lost it. I lay down in the sand and started bawling like a baby, or like a wife who has just lost her husband. I just felt a ripping inside me; and it was then I knew that to survive, to fully be alive, I had to get back the experience of the land and honor its rituals. The words *New Mexico* and *caretaker* came to me so strongly at that moment. Nothing like that had ever happened to me before, and I knew I was getting a message and had better listen.

So right then it became my quest to find a place to take care of in New Mexico, the Land of Enchantment. I loved my friends so much that it was hard for me to imagine I could stay away from them for longer than three or four months, but in my good-bye circle with them I cried and said, "When you see me next time, I'm not gonna be the same." A part of me knew I was coming back to self . . . knew I was dancing my way home.

It is eleven years later now. I have spent them in a special ritual of falling deeply and ever more deeply in love with my canyon home, with my beautiful soul mate Wolf, and with a self I never knew existed. From beneath the masks I once wore was revealed a woman as giving and strong as she was needy and vulnerable. A nurturing woman, feminine woman, a woman who loves her body and all its so-called imperfections. A woman who knows her home inside and out, running barefoot through river bottoms full of stickers and sharp rocks; who knows where the plants grow, which she can eat and which she can make tea with. A woman who knows her way, and has led other women barefoot up steep hills in the dark with no moon, no flashlights, bending close to the ground to feel which way the trail goes. (Is it over there? No, feel the ground with your toes—dance it! it's here!)

Yes, I've become a grounded woman, rooted to canyon soil, fed by its river, singing where I am heard by no judgmental ears. Singing to only my sister elk and graceful heron, bats and bobcats, mountain lion and coatimundi, to the raccoons and ringtail cats, skunks and swallows, hummingbirds and scorpions, rattlesnakes and bumblebees. I sing and dance to them my song of grounded celebration, my voice echoing off the canyon walls, the canyon singing back to me.

If I can "come down to earth," so can anyone. The connection that feeds me can feed you in a neighborhood backyard, or through a special rock you pick up off your altar. It isn't something you "get," because you already have it. You just need to feel it, pay attention to it, and then act out of that sacred center. We can find it in even the busiest moments—that sacred space, that sense of ritual that becomes a refuge of quiet vision and knowingness from which we can reach out, touching others most intensely and meaningfully, cuddling with the power and promises of the Earth, creating art and community, standing up to threats and defending what deserves defending. Grounded in being, in presence and place—we're sacred, flawless, and never alone. Hallelujah, we're home, and we're dancing!

getting closer to others and yourself

Here are some ways to help you think about your connection to the world around you.

- Notice what makes you feel more connected, and move toward that as quickly as you can. Notice what makes you feel more disconnected, more separate, more apart, and move away from that just as surely.
- Notice what things help take you out of your objectifying mind, and how the five senses make you feel a seamless part of everything that exists. Make every walk in the forest a chance to embrace the world, every bath a gateway to the all.
- Consider how empathy—feeling what other beings feel—can bring you closer to them.
- Trust your instincts and follow your intuition in the direction of ever greater belonging.
- Practice intimacy. Get close! Touch the world with your probing hands, your feeling heart, your hopes and prayers.
- Create an altar if you don't have one already, and fill it with things that represent and remind you of your connection to Earth, Spirit, and your magick.
- Use lovemaking as a means to leave separateness behind and voyage into blissful interconnectedness.
- Use pain the same way, as a bridge to all the hurting, sentient life forms of all time, and Mother Nature's (Gaia's) suffering over her vanished species, clear-cut forests, and unsung rivers.
- Find the joy of the living universe in every happy moment.
- Feel how the birds are an extension of you, as you are an extension of the Earth . . . and feel yourself singing through them.
- Feel how being connected to a purpose connects you to the purposeful flow of history and evolution, and to those who in future ages will give themselves to their own timely missions.
- Dance the Earth, and allow the Earth to dance you!

—Loba—

ELEMENTS: FROM A CHRISTIAN CONSECRATION RITUAL

AMBROSE HAWK

The works that follow incorporate classic principles of magick, which I feel would make them useful with only minor alterations to practitioners on other paths. A few words of explanation need to be given. All of these incantations were used in rituals for the consecration of objects. Not all of the elements would be appropriate for every ritual, obviously. The solar charge, for instance, is adapted from an ancient Coptic ritual for wisdom, and is best used on the solar points (the Sabbats) for a consecration. The first use was to consecrate a jar of honey as a base for healing potions—thus the references to honey within it.

Planetary charges would be appropriate only under particular circumstances. In ceremonial magick, many operations are best done at the appropriate planetary hour on the appropriate planetary day. On the other hand, many times there is a significant correspondence between some item and a certain planet. Crystal balls, for instance, are highly sensitive to the moon and to Mercury. Significant planetary aspects are also an important consideration, as the planetary energies are greatly increased by them. Full moon and new moon, for instance, are the opposition and conjunction, respectively, of the sun and the moon. Thus, when such a planetary influence happens on the day a ritual is performed, it is useful to access directly each of the involved planets in turn. To learn more about when each conjunction and opposition falls, get yourself a good astrological calendar.

The triangle of manifestation is formed by touching the thumbs and forefingers together. The triangle is formed slightly above the forehead, creating a nexus and a focus wherein the cosmic energies invoked can join and be patterned by the will and imagination of the mage.

The closing of the planetary charges was done in a typically Roman Catholic manner as well. Some people make the sign of the cross with a wand over the items to be charged. Many folks use some other gesture, such as an invoking pentagram or hexagram. This is followed by pushing the invoked energies with the wand (either a striking or a thrusting gesture) with the "Fiat!"—Latin for "Let it be done" or "So mote it be," but with a more imperative connotation, more like, "Do it!" The "Amen" has a similar meaning, but it contains the concept of established reality; thus the "Fiat!" followed by "Amen" is like saying, "So mote it be!" followed by, "So it is!" In my thinking, that rings of manifestation!

Blessing and Protection

Bless my space, O Lord! North, South, East, West;
My Lord brings me all things blest. East, West, South, North;
All shadow, our God's life drives forth.
South, North, West, East; Angels draw us to the bridal feast.
West, East, North, South; Let Wisdom's winds flow through my
   mouth.
From earth and sky, all evil fly, from blessed birth, in sky and earth.
From sea and fire, our foes retire. By fire and sea, comes Love to me.

A Charging

Holy Mighty One, whose high throne, beyond all worlds and stars
still stands;
To make thy children's dreams alive, command those Powers who
thee attend.

Hear us, Jesus, Brother, Lord; by your words of Love, we dare to ask
That Powers' bright eternal lights, live and act to aid our task.
Bless us, bright Spirits, with sacred song, to fill this space with
happy praise.
Look on these tools, shaped from our dreams; Live in power there,
all of our days.
Amen.

Incantation

By the holy names which I have named; By the holy names which I
have writ;
Come, ye Powers, which I have summoned! Be here, and do your
proper bit.
Though some passing fancy I may claim, some trifle like health or
wealth or fame;
It's my spirit's growth I most desire, to flame more brightly with
holy Fire.
So bring to none an undue harm, nor, with false blessing cursed,
charm.
Make this and me more magically strong, to share the joy of the
godly throng.
Amen. Fiat!

An Evocation of the Sun

AVE, DOMINUS! AVE, SOL INVICTUS!
Hail, Sun of righteousness, who shines upon all the land.
Come upon this [honey]; send your sacred Fire into it;
Contain it and reveal it in your holy light.
Manifest your rule above the twelve powers,
That this [honey] become the phane
Where your generosity shines upon our desires.

In the name of your great archangel, Abraxas,
Whose hand is stretched out over the primal rays of the
Cosmos, you must enlighten my heart.
Shine upon me that I may share your joy,
That I may perceive your wisdom.
Thank you, Y.H.V.H.: Holy Powerful One,
Holy Immortal One, Holy Wise and All-Knowing One.
Hail, bright and shining Star, for the joyful light you have shone
   upon me
Kairos, Kyrios! Light of gladness, light of the eons, light of joy,
Light of my eyes, lamp of my body, Y.H.V.H. Sabbaoth
Give me the sun as a garment and the moon for a cloak.
Carry me in the ship of the sun that I may sail through and over
The tempest of evil.
Assign to me the rulers of the great planets,
Their spirit, their intelligences, their mighty powers,
That I may share in the life of the stars
And be made worthy to behold your face.
As you love me you must give me your glory of the sun,
You of the great Number, that I be guarded from all evil.

Note that the text incorporates elements of similar prayers from Syrian
Coptic Christians of the second century. The original was found in Marvin
Meyer and Richard Smith, eds., *Ancient Christian Magic: Coptic Texts of Ritual
Power* (HarperSanFrancisco, 1994). This is a lovely compendium of magickal
texts surviving from about a two- or three-century span among the Egyptian
and Syrian Coptic Christians: it reveals, among other things, the comfort
early Christians had in blending magickal behavior with their spiritual life.

Evocation of the Planetary Powers

Jupiter

Make the triangle of manifestation;

ABA, by the love with which you sent your only begotten Son to be our salvation, so also in thy generosity send down Jophiel the intelligence of Jupiter, and Hismael the spirit of Jupiter.

Bring the triangle down onto the talisman:

Empower this kamea and seal of Jupiter, that through this talisman we might gain the resources material, emotional, mental, and spiritual to be also loving, generous, and blessed in this temporal life!

Spread your hands and take up the wand:

IN NOMINE PATRIS, ET FILII, ET SPIRITUS SANCTI. AMEN.
In the name of the Father, Son, and Holy Ghost. Amen.

Touch the talisman with the wand three times, saying,

FIAT! FIAT! FIAT!

Sun

Make the triangle of manifestation;

By the sacred signs of the ineffable Name: VAU, HEH; and by the holy Name, ELOH, the God most high, we call upon Nachiel the intelligence of the Sun, and Sorath the spirit of the Sun.

Bring the triangle down onto the talisman:

Empower this kamea and seal of the sun, the symbol of Sol Invictus, that through this talisman we might gain the resources material, emotional, mental, and spiritual to be also loving, generous, and blessed in this temporal life!

Spread your hands and take up the wand:

IN NOMINE PATRIS, ET FILII, ET SPIRITUS SANCTI. AMEN.
In the name of the Father, Son, and Holy Ghost. Amen.

Touch the talisman with the wand three times, saying,

FIAT! FIAT! FIAT!

The Moon

Make the triangle of manifestation;

> *By the mystic name, HOD; and the holy Name, Elim; we call upon Hasmodai the spirit of the moon, and schedbarschemoth Schartathan the spirit of the spirits of the moon, and Malcha Betharsisim Hed Beruah Schehalim the intelligence of the intelligences of the moon.*

Bring the triangle down onto the talisman and spread your hands:

> *Empower this kamea and seal of the moon, the sacred shield of our blessed and Virgin Mary, that through this talisman we might gain the resources material, emotional, mental, and spiritual to be also loving, generous, and blessed in this temporal life!*

Take up the wand:

> *IN NOMINE PATRIS, ET FILII, ET SPIRITUS SANCTI. AMEN.*
> *In the name of the Father, Son, and Holy Ghost. Amen.*

Touch the talisman with the wand three times, saying,

> *FIAT! FIAT! FIAT!*

Mars

Make the triangle of manifestation;

> *By the mighty names of God: He, Y.H.Y., and Adonai, we call upon Camael the archangel of Mars, and Graphiel its genius, and Barzabel its spirit, that they join with St. Michael, the archangel and captain of the hosts of heaven, even as are named by ELOHIM Sabbaoth.*

Bring the triangle down onto the talisman:

> *Empower this [kamea, seal, talisman] that we might gain strength and health and further the resources, whether material, spiritual, social, or emotional, to be also loving, generous, and blessed in this temporal life!*

Spread your hands and take up the wand:

> *IN NOMINE PATRIS, ET FILII, ET SPIRITUS SANCTI. AMEN.*
> *In the name of the Father, Son, and Holy Ghost. Amen.*

Touch the talisman with the wand three times, saying,

> *FIAT! FIAT! FIAT!*

Venus

Make the triangle of manifestation;

By the mystic and holy name A.H.A., by the holy name Shaddai El Chai, we call upon Hagiel the intelligence of Venus, and Kedemel the spirit of Venus, and by Bne Seraphim, the intelligences of Venus, that through the love of the Blessed Virgin and the power of Hanael the archangel,

Bring the triangle down onto the talisman:

Empower this talisman in this time of [season], that we in the plane of [Earth] might gain under the ministries of [angels of the season] the abundant resources not only to fill our material, emotional, mental, and spiritual needs but to be also loving, generous, and blessed in this temporal life!

Spread your hands and take up the wand:

IN NOMINE PATRIS, ET FILII, ET SPIRITUS SANCTI. AMEN.
In the name of the Father, Son, and Holy Ghost. Amen.

Touch the talisman with the wand three times, saying,

FIAT! FIAT! FIAT!

Mercury

Make the triangle of manifestation;

By the mystic and holy names, Asboga, Din, and Doni, we call upon Tiriel the intelligence of Mercury, and Tapthartharath the spirit of Mercury, that through the love of Hagia Sophia and the power of St. Raphael and St. Michael the archangels,

Bring the triangle down onto the talisman:

This [talisman] should receive power from this time of [season], that here in the plane of [Earth] it might gain under the ministries of [angels of the season] the power to inflame our minds and imaginations to understand and to express those things we need to gain abundant resources, not only to fill our material, emotional, mental, and spiritual needs but also to be loving, generous, and blessed even in this temporal life.

Spread your hands and take up the wand:

IN NOMINE PATRIS, ET FILII, ET SPIRITUS SANCTI. AMEN.
In the name of the Father, Son, and Holy Ghost. Amen.

Touch the talisman with the wand three times, saying,

FIAT! FIAT! FIAT!

Saturn

Make the triangle of manifestation;

> *By the mystic and holy names: AB, H-D, JAH, and HOD; and especially by the mighty Name of Y.H.V.H. ELOHIM, The Most High God, who says of himself, Eheiah Asher Eheiah: I am that I am; I call upon Cassiel, that mighty angel and ruler of Saturn, to direct Agiel the intelligence of Saturn and Zazel the spirit of Saturn to direct their virtues and powers into this work.*

Bring the triangle down onto the talisman:

> *That this [talisman] should receive power from this time of [season], that here in the plane of [Earth] it might gain under the ministries of [the angels of the season] the power to inspire us to meet the test and to protect our souls and our material beings and our emotional connections from harm: not only to fill our material, emotional, mental, and spiritual needs but also to be loving, generous, and blessed even in this temporal life!*

Spread your hands and take up the wand:

> *IN NOMINE PATRIS, ET FILII, ET SPIRITUS SANCTI. AMEN.*
> *In the name of the Father, Son, and Holy Ghost. Amen.*

For the dismissal, touch the talisman with the wand three times, saying,

> *All ye spirits whom I've addressed, these sacred bonds never burst:*
> *By God, these powers must be blest, for greatest good from last to first.*

As you can see, it's easy to work with the basic evocation and adjust it for each planet's energy.

FIRE SCRYING: SOPHIA'S LEGACY

CHRISTENA LINKA

It was a Thursday night in July 1971, and the moon was full. I did not realize that I was about to meet someone who would change my life.

Nels and Peter had started the fire in the pit they had dug the previous spring. The altar, which they had constructed from a large flat stone balanced on a huge boulder, stood a little to the north of the pit in the middle of the circle. Susan had brought her special Lady cakes and set them on a smaller rock that stood to the left of the altar. (Refusing to put a plate of food on the ground, she had insisted the men bring in a special table rock.)

Judith arrived, panting, with the wine. She had run up the hill to the glade to bring the first news of a guest. Breathless, she burst into the clearing: "Christena, Song-Weaver is bringing a girl!"

Just at that moment, Song-Weaver, my brother, walked into the glade, holding the hand of a girl so tiny, at first I thought she was one of the wee folk.

"This is Sophia," said Song-Weaver by way of introduction.

Her smile was warm, and her curly, short black hair seemed to dance around her beautiful oval face as we welcomed her.

The moon was up, and it was time to begin our full moon rite. At first, I watched Sophia whenever I could as she followed Song-Weaver's actions. I soon realized that she knew what our circle was about, so I relaxed into the moment. The circle seemed to have a special magick that night.

Later, the seven of us sat around the fire, sipping the last of the wine. No one was ready to break the enchantment of the night. The full moon was hanging low in the western sky, and the warm summer air was still. An owl hooted out of the darkness. Judith, a singer with a struggling rock band, put more wood on the now-dying embers of the fire. No one objected. We were not ready to leave the tranquillity of the glade. This had been an especially good Esbat. The sending of power had affected us all, putting us into deep reflection.

Susan was the first to speak.

"I see a horse galloping in the fire." Her voice held wonderment, unusual for down-to-earth, matter-of-fact Susan.

We all peered more intently into the fire, each of us finding visions dancing in the flames.

"It reminds me of seeing pictures in the fire at summer camp," I said.

"Yeah, we used to do this at Scout camp," chuckled Song-Weaver. "I was always seeing fire engines and Mounties. Stuff like that. I couldn't make up my mind if I wanted to be a fireman or join the RCMP." He gave a self-effacing snort as he glanced down at his slight frame.

Standing five feet, seven inches and weighing about 125 pounds, Song-Weaver did not have the physical build of a firefighter or a police officer. Turning toward him, Sophia slipped her arm protectively around his shoulders. "If you were built otherwise, you wouldn't be the weaver of songs," she said, her voice carrying a knowing authority.

Lifting her small chin, Sophia looked into the leaping flames. "My mother uses a candle flame to see into the future," she said in her soft voice. "I do it myself sometimes," she added, almost as an afterthought. Her dark curls framed her small head, creating a shining halo in the glow of the fire.

Nels and Peter, each standing over six feet, glanced at each other, rose up, walked around to Song-Weaver, and in one fluid movement bent down and picked him up.

"Come along little brother, we have some serious talking to do, down by the lake," said Nels, and they walked off carrying the laughing Song-Weaver between them.

We all love Song-Weaver for his sometimes crazy humor, his kind heart, and the beautiful music he creates. I had seen a special glow between him and Sophia, and I wondered if this was what Nels had on his mind.

With Song-Weaver carried off by Nels and Peter, Sophia turned and gazed into the fire. She seemed nice, though quiet and reserved. Because I had been leading the circle, I had not found the time for any conversation. Sophia intrigued me, and I wanted to get to know her better.

"Tell us about yourself, Sophia," I said.

"I came to Canada at the age of five, with my parents, from Italy. I am eighteen now."

Too young! She's twelve years younger than Song-Weaver, I thought.

Judith glanced sharply at me, as if she knew what I was thinking, and abruptly said, "Have you ever been to a Witches' circle before?"

"Well, not quite like this," faltered Sophia. Her eyes seemed to get larger, and I saw her take a deep breath and gulp. Speaking in a husky voice, she added, "I've always done rituals with my family." She then lapsed into silence, staring into the fire.

Susan, always a gentle soul, reached out and stroked Sophia's bent head. Speaking softly, she said, "Don't let Judith get to you. Perhaps you'd like to tell us about your family."

"Well," began Sophia, "my grandmother in Italy is known for her healing potions, and can lift the evil eye. My mother is known for the predictions she makes by looking into the flame of a candle. I have never told her that I do it too, but I think she knows. My father works in construction. He knows everything there is to know about tile and marble, I think."

"Tell us more about this candle scrying, if that's what you call it," Judith demanded, her sharp eyes looking directly at Sophia.

No longer intimidated by Judith's forceful approach, Sophia explained. "Candle scrying is a good name for it. I've never heard it referred to by any name, but my mother does it in front of the Lare."

"What the heck is a *larr ray*? Some sort of fish?" demanded Judith in her most aggressive manner.

I told Judith to shut up.

Sophia was unfazed by Judith's outburst as she calmly continued. "A Lare is a shrine," she said. "Because we are Italian, most people think the Lare is a Catholic shrine, but it is far older than Catholicism. The small statue in the shrine represents our ancestors, and my mother believes that they help her to see the future. We have strong family traditions that go back generations. My family would be horrified if they knew that I called myself a Witch." She smiled, then added, "But really, that is what we are, Witches. My family, I mean."

"Please, tell us how to do the candle scrying," spoke up Susan.

"It is always best to prepare yourself for any magickal work by first cleansing your body. I make my own bath oil from essential oils, using five parts lemongrass oil and two parts basil oil. This aids in the relaxation process for successful divination," Sophia said. "After cleansing my body, I dress in comfortable, loose-fitting clothing."

Smiling across the fire toward Judith, she said, "You don't want your body to feel restricted," as if she knew Judith's passion for freedom of movement. "It is always best to wear a natural fabric such as cotton, silk, or soft wool," she added.

Turning again toward Susan, she said, "Choose a place where you will be undisturbed and unplug the phone. It is okay to have some soft music playing if you wish, but I think that it is better at first to have your surroundings as quiet as possible."

She then focused on the fire, her eyes taking on a dreamy quality as she continued to speak. "When I work with the candle, I first cast the circle. Place your taper candle in front of you in a tall candleholder if you have one, or put it on your altar and sit on the floor in front of it. You will want it to be at eye level. Sit in a comfortable and relaxed upright position, and you are ready to begin. Relax your body, allowing any physical tension to dissolve. Become conscious of your breathing, but do not try to change its rhythm; just keep breathing in and out in a natural flow. Let your eyes focus on the flame of your candle."

Her breathing changed to a deep, relaxed rhythm as she went on. "Consider your thoughts now, without trying to impede them. Take note of your mood and allow your thinking to drift along with it. Now quietly push aside any intruding thoughts and simply be silent. Concentrate on the flame of the candle. With practice, you will become calm. Remember to keep breathing in a natural and relaxed manner, while clearing your mind of all thoughts. When you become calm within, you are ready to direct your inner energy to wherever you desire. You are now ready to focus on what it is you wish to know."

Sophia's voice took on a deeper tone and her breathing slowed again as she continued. "Half-close your eyes and relax, staring into the flame. Become quiet within. I guess you would say "grounded." It may take some practice to instill the calm within, but soon the pictures will come. It will happen. Like scrying with a mirror or water, the candle is just another tool," she added.

Sophia looked directly at Judith. "You only have to open yourself to the experience. You can also use this technique as a kind of ritual to restore balance, and bring about any changes you may wish to make in your life."

Never able to stay quiet for long, Judith asked, "What do you mean, *changes?*"

"We could all do with a little change in our attitudes, our ways of thinking," Sophia said quietly. "I know you are a good person at heart, Judith, but you get forceful and loud when you could find more empathy from others by being still and quiet. I think you are afraid to let people get too close to you, so you push them away. Are you afraid of being rejected and hurt?" Much to the surprise of both Susan and myself, Judith brushed her hand over her eyes and nodded silently to Sophia.

We knew that Judith, besides being sidesplittingly funny, could be brash and sometimes downright rude. We had thought we knew why Judith maintained her aggressive manner. Her single mother, who worked as a cleaning lady, had raised her to become strongly independent. Judith's ambition came from a childhood of penny-pinching. She had held an after-school paper route from the age of eleven until high school. In high school there were various after-school jobs, as well as full-time summer jobs that had left little time for teenage friendships to develop.

At twenty-four, Judith still lived with her mother and had yet to realize her ambition to work in advertising. Her father was an unknown entity, and she never referred to him. Neither Susan nor I had ever thought that she could, or would, change. She was just good old Judith, the laughing punster, to us. Sophia had seen something in Judith that we had not. Underneath her boisterous ways, Judith was afraid.

Sophia looked again into Judith's face as she spoke. "See the fire and look into the dancing golden orange flame. Watch as it burns. Connect to the feeling of wondrous power within you, and you will know your destiny."

Judith's lip quivered slightly as she asked, "How do I do that?"

"Well, you might ask, 'How can I express the gifts I was born with?'" suggested Sophia. "Set your goal to recognize your gift of power and your vision for the future. Think about how you can use your marvelous energy in attaining that which you desire. Know that you have within you the ability to achieve greatness. Know that you will benefit greatly by learning patience. Seek to become ever conscious of the self, allowing your heart to rule. Know that your spiritual fire is ever burning within."

Judith's face took on a look of pure serenity as Sophia's soft, husky voice continued. "Within your spiritual self you will know that as you add the fuel of your heart's desire to your inner fires, you create your destiny. See the flame take on the shape of that which you desire. As you meet obstacles in your life, learn to call them teacher, and friend. As you are tested you will find the power to avert defeat."

Grinning at Sophia, Judith said, "I've got to learn to be more patient, eh?"

Sophia answered, "Learn patience, for it is your wisest counsel."

We sat quietly for a long time, each deep in thought, gazing into the fire. Susan was the first to break the silence. "How did you get so wise for one so young?"

"I listened to my grandmother," answered Sophia.

"Any words of wisdom for me?" asked Susan. "I am a nurse, and I've always wanted to specialize in neonatal medicine. I would need more schooling, and I'm twenty-nine with two children. Could I handle the stress if I decide to take more training?"

"Let me hold your hands for a minute," said Sophia. As she gazed into the flames, a mystical look crossed her face. "I see you as a perfectionist, so it will be hard for you to admit any weaknesses. You already know your strengths," she said, smiling. "Your mind is that of an intellectual with a very practical nature. This can serve you well in many enterprises throughout life. Learn not to escape from reality by denying what is happening. You must develop acceptance and learn that failure is also a teacher of the lessons of life. You may not win, but you will never lose, for you will always learn from what takes place."

Sophia paused, and then continued. "Seeing into your inner self you will become aware that success lies in contacting your intuitive knowing. Set your goal to learn to be attuned to your own rhythms."

She paused again, her eyes taking on a faraway look. "Ah," she said, "you have a natural psychic ability. This will lead you to a wonderful sense of fulfillment in helping others. Use it first to look within, become aware of your consciousness. Learn to take care of your spiritual needs, and get to know your emotions. You will then walk the path of the psychic healer."

Susan's face flushed and she leaned away from the fire, deep in her own thoughts.

Turning toward me and raising one arched eyebrow, Sophia looked at me questioningly.

"Okay, let me have it," I said, suddenly afraid of what she would say.

Sophia took both my hands in hers and gazed again into the fire for what seemed like a very long time. Then she spoke: "Know that you are now ready to accomplish what it is that you want for your life. Avidly seek to change, for it is your salvation. Your goal is to realize your gift of innate honesty, and to use it within, to know yourself. Be observant of your growth of will and self-rule, and know that your spiritual self will grow strong when you have the willingness to nourish others."

Turning slightly, she looked directly into my eyes as she said, "Learn to understand how to use your abilities to teach and communicate with others around you. In sharing your ideas with others, you will find that you are not alone. You must become more aware and exercise only positive thoughts. You are an eager explorer of life. Your strength is like that of a strong tree, but you must learn to bend with the winds of change to achieve all that you can. Recognize that your inner strength gives lasting freedom."

She lapsed into silence as we heard the men returning.

"Have we got any towels here?" yelled Peter from the path.

"The lake is warm tonight," called out Nels, with Song-Weaver following close on his heels as they entered the glade.

Song-Weaver slipped between us and put his arm around Sophia's shoulder. I heard him whisper, "You've been turning on your special magick."

Sophia smiled.

Sophia and Song-Weaver were married at Lammas 1972, and they spent many happy years together until Sophia passed into the Summerland in 1998.

That night was the beginning of Sophia's legacy to us. Her fearless, open honesty was like a fresh ocean breeze. She never referred to her family's practices as Witchcraft or the Strega. She seemed to have no name for it. Neither she, nor any one else in her family, had ever heard of Aradia, much less read *Aradia*. Nevertheless, from what she told us this night and on subsequent nights, the Old Religion was exactly what her family had practiced for generations.

Over the years, Sophia taught us all a great deal about the Old Religion, about life, and about courage. She helped Judith become sure of herself and less prone to verbal outbursts of volcanic proportions. When Judith's rock 'n' roll career faltered, she grew out of her hippie stage. She followed Sophia's sage advice to attain her dream of working in the business world. She started on the bottom rung in advertising, and using her ambition and drive, she now has an executive position in Vancouver.

Under Sophia's tutelage, Susan learned how to use her psychic abilities and became a neonatal nurse. Susan is now a grandmother and midwife in Ontario. She stays in touch and is still involved with the Craft.

Sophia taught me that I can learn just as much from someone a decade younger as from a person a decade older. She taught us all to be still, and listen, so we can learn. This is her legacy.

interpreting fire

Honor Sophia by trying your hand at fire scrying. For this activity you'll need a candle in a stable container. Dim the lights in the room where you're working, then light your candle with a specific question in mind. Focus your thoughts on the flame, then watch its behavior. You can begin interpreting the flame's movements by using these general guidelines:

- Dancing flames that are clear and bright mean a yes or positive answer, especially for health.
- Pale or small flames are an iffy answer that portends decrease, illness, or rough weather in your future
- A blazing flame (sudden) is a warning to watch for messages, eruptions in temper, or a "hot" situation.
- Colored flames are a sign to use the color correspondences (yellow for communication matters, red for passion, blue for spirits, and so on).
- A candle that will not light means a no or negative omen.
- Loud crackling or popping signals a cool reception (unfriendly atmosphere).
- Smoldering means resentment and animosity (often unexpressed).
- Twin flames signify multiple options, or divided interests or energies.
- An active flame stands for change.

You may want to record your divinations in your spiritual diary.

—Patricia Telesco—

GODDESS

ROWAN HALL

I am not one to overspiritualize my experiences, but some things happen in life that bolster faith and make "magick" far more real. For me, such an event happened at a Florida Pagan Gathering event in Boyd Hill, Florida, during a Beltane celebration. I was working as a guardian at that event. The main ritual was to be of two parts, a maypole dance and a meeting with an invoked goddess.

At the time, I was really skeptical about the invoked goddess part, figuring that the woman acting as the vessel would be just that—acting. Boy, was I wrong! I knew the woman personally—she follows a Hindu path—and I had heard from her mate that she intended to invoke the Hindu goddess Uma. *Yeah, right,* was my initial cynical thought.

As the ritual progressed, I discovered that the Goddess isn't afraid to make herself known. When the priestess passed me in procession to the main ritual circle, the hairs on the back of my neck stood up. Whatever or whoever was looking out of her eyes was *not* the woman I knew. The expression on her face was one of utter joy and wonder, and I knew that I was fixin' to have my world rocked!

During the ritual, those interested in speaking with the Goddess were to stand in line, so I took my place with all the rest. Time passed slowly, and I stepped out of line several times from boredom. I was in the process of walking completely away when one of the handmaidens indicated that it was my turn.

I politely waited for the man ahead of me to walk away, and then started heading for her dais. But I hadn't taken two steps when suddenly I found myself on my knees, sobbing—for what I was approaching was not, to my shock, a friend pretending to be a goddess, but rather, Goddess inhabiting the body of a friend! I can't explain how I knew, but my body crawled to her, and I found my head in her lap, while I sobbed out, "It's been so long!"

She spoke words to me that surrounded me and infused me. The specifics of the experience were lost—but it was an experience I will treasure for the rest of my life. I wanted to stay kneeling at her feet forever, but reality beckoned and I moved on to allow another to take my place.

I later found out that my personal reaction was not unusual: many people had been similarly shocked and so affected. More important, there were real lessons here for me—namely, that magick really does happen, and gods really can be invoked. And because of that awareness I offer two bits of wisdom. Be *very* careful of what you ask for, magickally; and don't invoke that which you cannot uninvoke, because it's real.

Honoring Deity

For those of you who work with Deity, if you haven't found a way to honor that Being in the ritual of your life on a daily basis, now is an excellent time to start. Above and beyond tending your altar, do you light a candle? Do you offer a prayer? Do you talk to Deity when you're cooking, gardening, or cleaning? Working with the gods and goddesses is all about relationship building, and that doesn't happen just by putting a statue on your altar or reading one book.

I also recommend keeping a special diary for your experiences throughout your process of working with and honoring Deity. For one thing, there will be moments like Rowan's that you will not want to forget. For another, you can return to this diary as a source of inspiration, insights, and hope again and again.

—Patricia Telesco—

USING PAGAN RITUAL IN THE REAL WORLD

MARGOT ADLER

A lmost twenty-three years ago, I led a Pagan ritual for non-Pagans that had a lasting effect on bonds of friendship and community. The experience made me rethink the power of ritual in the mundane world. Most of us involved with Paganism and Wicca have experienced powerful and ecstatic ceremonies within our own communities; many of us have also seen ritual used in political work—the kind of rituals Starhawk and others do at demonstrations and civil-disobedience actions. But it is rare for us to experience Pagan rituals in the ordinary world. Often, when I look around my office and watch the complex interactions of the people who work there, I think, *Wouldn't a circle be great to resolve this situation?* or *Suppose we all sat around and did this exercise, wouldn't it clear the air?* So I want to tell the story of one simple ritual that succeeded beyond my expectations.

How It Happened

In the fall of 1981, I moved away from New York City for a year, because I had a Nieman fellowship at Harvard University. The fellowship is awarded to journalists to come and study anything they want for year. It's a dream chance to be at college with none of the downsides: we were able to audit almost any course, and we had to do the papers or exams in only one course per semester. Even more important, we were old enough to have put away the torments and baggage of adolescence. Several afternoons a week there were seminars where writers, thinkers, and politicians came to talk. Even more amazing, our spouses got the same perks we did.

Looking back at my college experience in the 1960s, I realize I was too tense to allow myself much fun, too uptight to socialize comfortably. There is a famous quotation by T. H. White: "I arise every morning torn between the desire to save the world and the desire to savor the world. It makes it hard to plan the day." In those days, I was so determined to help save the world and still be an excellent student that I had little time to savor it. And let's face it, few humans are really comfortable in their own skin before they reach thirty. The Nieman fellowship allowed me to have the joy and freedom of university life in the comfort of adulthood.

While it was intellectually a blast (among other things, I took ancient Greek and a course in religion at the divinity school with Diana Eck), socially it was like finding your carcass. I had always been an outsider, and suddenly I was spending a year with some forty people (the eighteen Niemans, various spouses, and kids) in a constant round of conversation, dinners, and glasses of cheap champagne.

But this all took place only a year and a half after the publication of my book, *Drawing down the Moon,* so the persistent question was how to share my Pagan and Wiccan beliefs with my newfound family. Like most people I have encountered in the mundane world, even if they knew about my beliefs, they never asked.

So a few days before the end of our fellowship year, I decided to hold a ritual. I called it "a ceremony to cement our bonds as a community, and to call for protection for those going into dangerous places." This was no joke; several of the journalists were going to war zones.

I knew the ritual had to be simple, with almost no paraphernalia to scare them off. I chose a couple of easy chants that have gone around the Pagan community for decades:

> We are an old people,
> We are a new people,
> We are the same people,
> Deeper than before

This chant seemed eerily appropriate since we had all spent a year away from our jobs, rethinking our lives, experimenting, and taking intellectual risks. The other chant was an old favorite with both Pagan and Eastern religious groups:

> Listen, listen, listen—to my heart's song,
> I will never forget you; I will never forsake you.
> I will never forget you; I will never forsake you.

This also was right for the group because we came from all over the world, had bonded quickly, and now were saying good-bye as we returned to our jobs and responsibilities.

I put up notices that the ritual would take place in the late afternoon, two days before the end of our fellowship year. I brought a wand, some elemental symbols, a goblet, and some wine. I was very nervous.

Who Came

More men came than women, and more spouses came than fellows. I wondered if the women felt threatened. Most of the women were single and had perhaps been forced to make a choice between career and family. Perhaps the men had more of a sense of entitlement, and as a result were more comfortable and more able to avail themselves of an experience outside the norm.

There were about fifteen people at the ritual. We stood in a circle, and I told them a tiny bit about Nature spirituality. I asked them to imagine a blue flame circling around them all and told them that we were creating a place sacred and apart from the mundane world. I did a simple invocation to Air, Fire, Water, and Earth, and then asked each person present to say one thing that had changed for them because of the year that had passed. A crusty war reporter from Europe said he had become more optimistic about life; a man in his thirties said he had started cooking. A woman talked about changing her career. We slowly went around the circle. After the first chant, I did an invocation for protection for the journalists going into places of turmoil. I poured the wine, sprinkled a few drops on the ground, and thanked the Earth for her blessings. The goblet was passed around, and everyone said a few words of thanks. We ended the ritual with "Listen, listen, listen," and a very simple closing.

The Aftereffects

After everyone left, I wondered what it had all meant. Had it "worked"? What effect did it have? The next morning, one of the women who had attended—and who lived in the apartment across the hall—knocked on my door. She'd had the strangest dream, she said. She dreamed that she had been reborn from the womb.

The next day we had our official farewell ceremony and lunch at a Boston restaurant. We were all dressed formally, and at the end of the meal there were many toasts. Suddenly, spontaneously, two people who had been in the ritual stood up. Then it was four, and suddenly everyone was linking hands around the room in one big circle. Everybody began to sing, "Listen, listen, listen—to my heart's song" in the middle of the restaurant. As the song began to soar, and as those who had not attended the ritual became familiar with the words, two of the men in our group began sobbing uncontrollably. The song went on and on, mixed with hugs and embraces.

We all went back to our lives, and most of us went back to our old jobs. Six years later I got married and I sent invitations to all the fellows and their families. A surprising number came—from Italy, from Kentucky, from New York and Boston and Washington, D.C. Now it is twenty-three years later, but we have not lost touch. We have had reunions and minireunions and informal gatherings, and of course email. I consider many members of this group among my closest friends to this day.

What Did It All Mean?

In thinking about this experience, I have come to believe that simple ritual can bring to the surface that which is hidden. It can make conscious the unconscious. We had all experienced a remarkable year—we had forged new friendships, experienced new ideas. But few of us had said any of this aloud, and there are not many ways to talk about these things in our culture. So we partied and had dinners and good conversation, but we had never said to one another, "Your friendship is important to me. Our conversations are healing, and I am rethinking the way I want to live my life." Our simple ritual allowed these thoughts to come to the surface. It allowed two of the men who didn't usually express much emotion to express powerful feelings publicly. The ritual even entered a woman's dreams, and it allowed a group of people to make an outward commitment to one another that they might not have done in the same way without the ceremony to crystallize their feelings. I am not saying that we would not be friends, but our class of 1982 has stayed closer than many other fellowship years, and the friendships that were created have remained a permanent part of our lives. I am convinced the ritual helped make that happen.

Ever since that event, I look at the mundane world differently. I know that we can take the tools that we use in the Pagan and Wiccan traditions and find ways to use them in the larger community, and in the workplace. The ritual technology that we use in our spiritual life can have a powerful impact beyond the small bubble that is our community. It can help create powerful bonds in the larger world. The only thing each of us needs is the courage to take the first steps.

SOUND

KRISTIN MADDEN

Imagine a perfect moment—a point in time when you are filled with joy, harmony, and balance. You are surrounded by loving, supportive people, and your energies merge together to manifest the perfect beauty of All That Is. Your senses are attuned to the sound of magick flowing through you and through the group as a whole. And it is the most amazing music you have ever heard. It speaks directly to your heart, body, and spirit as it transforms that moment into pure perfection.

One of the things I love best about Pagan community is the opportunity for these moments to manifest spontaneously. They are everywhere, and the purity of bliss I experience through them has brought me pleasure, connection, inspiration, and healing. The magick of sound is something so subtle yet so powerful that we often overlook it.

Did you know that the sense of hearing is one of the last senses to fade when our physical bodies die? Even people in comas or under anesthesia often report memories of things that were said to them when most other senses and abilities were suppressed. Many studies have been done on the healing effects of drumming and other forms of music.

The magick of sound is present throughout Pagan community. We sing circle songs, intone sacred sounds, play all kinds of instruments, and drum, drum, drum. Just being in the presence of such powerful sounds is transformative.

For me, it all began with song. As a child, I loved music and learned to play nearly every instrument in the school band. My longtime flute playing always connected me more deeply with Krishna, a deity I fell in love with when I was nine. But I found that sacred song gently lifted my energies and lulled me into trance. As I got older, I also found that it was not a good idea to listen to my favorite chants while driving— I often didn't realize I had passed my exit off the highway by many miles!

I have vivid memories of my first gong meditation. I was with my parents at a metaphysical festival in the mid 1980s and our dear friend, a Sikh and kundalini yoga master, led us in early morning *sadhana* followed by a gong meditation. Much like a shamanic journey, it was not led by any words . . . just the incredible vibration of the gong. I felt my entire body energize as I entered the most profound trance I had experienced to that point. I was glowing for days.

Now it is all about drums. While I had played drums as a teenager, the magick of rhythm never really hit me until I experienced a Pagan drum circle with African drums. It only took one circle and I was hooked. Fortunately, my husband is also hooked, and we don't often argue about which is more important—another drum or groceries.

As I write, this, I happily listen to my son practicing his *djembe* in the next room. I drummed while pregnant with him, and he has fallen asleep countless times to the rhythm of drum circles. At a young age, he learned that music has a way of bringing people together. In a drum circle, all different people connect on a spiritual level. People who might never become friends are united through music. Often local gatherings include harpists, saxophone players, singers, dancers, and more. Drummers of many different abilities play a wide variety of drums. And we are family, right then and there. We support one another rhythmically, and our energies mesh to create a musical entity of love and joy that is far beyond any of us. Life is good!

In drum healing workshops, I teach people to listen for overtones and any changes in the sound of the drum. Often these changes or additional tones are not truly auditory. We "hear" them because we are tuned in on a much deeper level than usual. During healing drum circles, people hear the music of orchestras. A healer-in-training will hear a distinct change in the sound of the drum at a point when energy is needed, even though observers (and often even the "patient") may not notice anything at all.

Once tuned in, people often report hearing songs and chants in the middle of a forest, at the seashore, and when touching a special stone. They become aware of the harmonies in birdsong, in the rain on a roof, and in the footsteps on a crowded city street. Sound exists beyond physical reality, and it has the power to bring great magick into our lives.

The specific type of music and instrument we resonate with is unique to each of us, but the magick is the same. Music transports us away from the mundane into a place of pure experience. It opens the doors to our own creativity and our innate connections with All That Is. Sound allows us to remember the harmonies present in life and the natural rhythms of all things.

So what is it for you? Do you sway to the sound of the flute, or do the drums make your body move? Does the crystal bowl send you into trance, or is it the slow, simple intonation of a few sounds? Or perhaps you are someone who hears the melodies of the water and air?

sound awareness

Try this to see what magickal sounds you can find in everyday life. Wherever you are right now, take a deep breath and relax. If possible, close your eyes and listen to your heartbeat. Can you feel it as well? Feel the beating of your heart connect you with the pulse of life, to the heartbeat of Mother Earth. Now focus on your hearing and listen to the sounds around you. What do you hear?

At first, it may sound like a jumble of disconnected noise, but keep listening with an awareness of the pulse of life you just connected to. Listen as the sounds mesh to form a unique type of music. Don't try to force a rhythm onto what you hear, just allow the sounds to give form to their own energy. What is your part in this music?

Later on, go into a natural place, perhaps a park or wilderness area. Try the same exercise there. If you had difficulty hearing a rhythm in town, try it again after experiencing the music of Nature. Be aware of how your judgments affect your experience of the rhythm you hear.

Practice this exercise everywhere in your life. Can you feel the music in eating, showering, working? Whenever it is safe to do so, allow your body to feel and move to that music. How does this affect your experience of the world, of life, and of your own body?

Our world is filled with sound, and that sound can become music to anyone's ears. Once you tune in to the music around you, you allow yourself to be joyful and free no matter where you are. You may have had a rotten day at work or school when you decide to roll down your window on the way home. At first the traffic, wind, or rain, or your tires on the pavement are just another irritant. Then suddenly they become a harmonious rhythm to your ears. When you give in to it, the day's events seem to fade away as the music carries you beyond it all. Your entire energy changes, and you feel like a new person. That is the moment of perfection, and an awareness of sound can make any moment magickal.

—Kristin Madden—

HEALING, SPELLS, AND OTHER SUNDRIES

PART OF THE "CRAFT" OF THE CRAFT IS illustrated beautifully in these contributions, which range from how to make a ring of protection to using tarot for healing. The modern metaphysical practitioner must, of need, be somewhat creative in approaching the world. It is not the same place in which our ancestors lived. The ongoing process of adaptation can leave us a bit breathless. Here are some magickal ideas on how to handle money, love, and even the common cold.

BLESSING AND PROTECTION

JUDITH LEWIS

These are some of my favorite protection and blessing recipes, which I frequently use in my own home and practices.

Protection

This a ritual for creating a ring of protection. If possible, perform this ritual on the first day of the three days of the full moon in the hour of Jupiter. Here are the items you'll need:

Dragon's Blood incense
Purple candle
Salt
Shell with water in it
Purple fabric
Red sandalwood
Purple ribbon
Silver ring you intend to wear

In your magickal space, light the Dragon's Blood incense and place it in the east, the candle in the south, the salt and the shell with water in it in the west, and the fabric with the sandalwood wrapped in it in the north with the ribbon close by.

Take the silver ring and face the east with the incense in front of you. Pass the ring through the smoke of the incense three times and say, "To the realms of Findias, I send my plea. I ask for the power of magick from thee. Protection from harm, your power to give; I ask for this now, so that I may live—free from harm."

Take the silver ring and face the south with the purple candle in front of you. Pass the ring through the heat of the flame three times and say, "To the realms of Gorias, I send my plea. I ask for the power of protection from thee. Protection from all who would raise a hand; against them all I beg power to stand—free from harm."

Take the silver ring and face the west with the shell with water in it and the salt beside it. Take three pinches of salt and place them in the water. Take the ring and stir the salt into the water by making three circles in the water while saying, "To the realms of Murias, I send my plea. I ask for protection and power from thee. Protection and safety all stored in this ring. Please come from your realms, protection you bring—keeping me safe."

Take the silver ring and face the north with the purple fabric with the sandalwood in it and the ribbon nearby. Stir the sandalwood with the ring three times and say, "To the realms of Falias, I send my plea. I ask for the magick of dragons from thee. Dragons who coil and leap to and fro, protecting me from harm wherever I go—keeping me safe."

Wrap the ring up in the fabric and tie it shut with the ribbon. Place the bundle on your altar or in a safe place for three days. Once the three days are up, remove the ring and either burn the sandalwood, fabric, and ribbon or dispose of them in a free-running stream.

Wear your ring whenever you feel you need protection.

General Blessing (Anointing Oil)

For general anointing purposes; this oil can be used in a spell of healing or protection to add power to the spell.

1   2-dram (10 ml) clean amber or cobalt glass vial
6   drops sandalwood Mysore essential oil
3   drops oakmoss essential oil
2   drops frankincense essential oil
1   drop myrrh essential oil
     amber resin or crystal
     Apricot kernel oil (has vitamin E for preservation)

Add the essential oils to the bottle and swirl them gently in order to get them blended. To charge the crystal, place it between your hands and concentrate hard on your intention. Add the crystal (make sure it is clean), and then add enough of the base oil to top the bottle off. (I don't use crystals in all my blends, but some people add crystals to their magickal blends to keep them charged with a specific intention.) Make sure you keep the prepared oil stored away from light and write on a sticker the name of the blend, time, date, moon phase, planetary hour, and any other information you wish so that you know what you made and when for use later.

Be careful as these blends will eventually go off (usually after about eight to twelve months). Use your nose and be aware of what each blend should smell like. If these blends are exposed to heat or light, they will degrade far more quickly, which also turns the magick. Once the mixture seems off, you can discard it, clean the bottle, and start a fresh batch. Be sure no trace of the previous blend remains, however, or your new one will smell rancid straight away. Essential oils are volatile, so bottles left with tops off will soon lose their potency. Ensure that oils don't get too hot and, in the case of citrus-based oils, not too cold. To test your essential oils to see if they are pure, put a drop or two on blotter paper. Genuine essential oils will evaporate completely, leaving no oily residue, though some will leave a color.

Candle Blessing Oil

This is a general-purpose oil that can be charged with different intentions by adding different crystals to the mix. Use rose quartz for love spells, amethyst for spells relating to psychic ability or astral travel, or other stones to charge the mix for your spell. I recommend colored-glass vials because clear ones don't seem to help the blends last as long.

1	1-dram (5 ml) clean amber or cobalt glass vial
6	drops sandalwood Mysore essential oil
4	drops frankincense essential oil
2	drops myrrh essential oil
2	drops lemon essential oil
	Citrine crystal
	Grapeseed oil

To prepare, follow the instructions for the anointing oil, above.

Self-Blessing Oil

For blessing yourself before rituals. Put a drop on your finger and draw a pentacle on your forehead while concentrating on clearing negativity from your aura. Warning: Some people are sensitive to lemon. Test this recipe on the inside of your elbow and leave for a few hours before using it anywhere else.

1	2-dram (10 ml) clean amber or cobalt glass vial
2	drops lemon essential oil
4	drops sandalwood Mysore essential oil
1	drop frankincense essential oil
2	drops ylang ylang essential oil
	Amethyst crystal
	Apricot kernel oil (has vitamin E for preservation)

To prepare, follow the instructions for the anointing oil, above.

Altar Incense

Burn as a general incense on the altar to purify it and to promote higher consciousness during rituals. This can also be used for spells of protection to enhance the protective energies of a place. Cinnamon oil is corrosive, so please be careful if you use it.

- 4 parts frankincense
- 3 parts myrrh
- 4 parts damar
- 3 parts sandalwood chips soaked in cinnamon oil, or hand-crushed cinnamon bark

To create the incense, choose how you will measure your ingredients— so if you want four parts of frankincense, will you use grams, ounces, pinches, or what? Once you have decided how much of each ingredient to use, you should grind coarse materials together somewhat finely: you want to be able to tell what each piece is, but also you want a small scoop to have all the different ingredients in it.

Mix everything together, but keep in mind that any blend that includes resins with oils will get gooey if stored for a long time and may bond together. If using sandalwood chips soaked in oil, let them dry out before blending, or blend only what you need as you need it.

Self-Blessing Incense

Use this incense for rituals of self-initiation or self-blessing, or anytime you feel you need a boost in your rituals.

- 5 parts frankincense
- 2 parts dried vervain leaves
- 3 parts gum arabic
- 1 part cedar
- 1 part cinnamon
- 3 parts sandalwood chips
- 3 parts sandarac

To prepare, follow the instructions for the altar incense, above.

CHRISTMAS STORY

TERRILYN

I have been practicing the Craft for thirteen years now, and three years before that was spent studying my Native American ways. I have always felt that casting spells for myself was selfish. A healing spell for another or teaching spellcasting to my covens was acceptable, but for myself I always preferred to work through life's challenges without the help of casting—that is, until one Christmas.

About seven years ago, I was a single working mom raising three sons. I celebrated both Christmas for them and Yule for myself. Two weeks before Christmas, everything I owned seemed to be breaking—washer, hot water heater, sump pump, dishwasher, furnace. My savings account was drained, and not one present under the tree for my boys. Talk about desperate! I couldn't let my children wake up to no presents under the tree. I knew I was going to have to have some help.

So the first night I did all my homework on when and how to do the spell I needed, and then I wrote it. A couple of days later, on a Friday, when I was ready to cast and had all the supplies I was going to need, I sent my sons to spend the night with a friend. I wanted time to prepare myself and not to be interrupted by a thousand questions either. I have never hidden from them who and what their mother is, but at times such as this I needed to be able to concentrate. Once their busy bodies had been sent on their overnight adventure, it was time for me to begin mine.

The day of a ritual, or almost any time I am working with the Spirits/God and Goddess, I try to fast and most definitely stay away from salt, which really tends to hinder my concentration. I also take a relaxing shower and listen to a meditation CD. My favorite has soft music combined with songs of whales and dolphins. I light the whole house with candles, climb in the shower, and prepare. I imagine myself in my place of power, allowing the sounds, the dance of light, and the water to cleanse me.

For supplies, I had two green candles with my sons' names written on one and "money" written on the other; and a green cloth with chamomile, lavender, catnip, and a tonka bean, with a gold ribbon for tying it up. I was now ready to cast.

I cast my circle and called the quarters as I normally do. (Almost everyone has a certain way of casting that they are comfortable with, so anyone who wants to try this spell should do it in their own way.) I placed both of the candles on my altar, with the cloth containing the herbs lying flat between them. While lighting the candles, I chanted the following and envisioned the money I needed coming to me:

Green as grass
The color of money
For which I ask
No more
No less
For the need of this plea
For the good of all
With no harm to come
So mote it be.

While chanting this, I took some of the wax from both candles and dripped it onto the herbs on the cloth. Then I tied the cloth up with the gold ribbon.

I thanked the God and Goddess and closed the circle, then left the candles burning while I feasted. The pouch went under my pillow, and I slept on it for seven nights—every night envisioning the money coming to me. At the end of the seven days I built a fire in my fire pit and burned the pouch—that comes from my Native American teachings of the smoke carrying a person's dreams to the Great Ones.

What happened for me? Exactly ten days after that spell and three days before Christmas (Yule), I received a check in the mail for four hundred dollars. It came from a company I had been employed by almost ten years before. It had been sold to another investor, and the money was in a retirement fund that I didn't even know about! It turned out to be a wonderful Christmas for my boys. The lesson I learned was that if the intent is pure and a true need exists, I do not need to feel selfish for spellcasting.

THE GIFTING WAY: HOW ABUNDANCE CAME TO ME

TAMARACK SONG

The "good life"—our culture's ideal way of living—is hopelessly out of reach for the vast majority of its people. Yet that doesn't keep the majority of people from trying to achieve it. We will spend most of a lifetime focused on such goals as home ownership, financial security, and collecting consumer goods. The dark side of that pursuit is most of a lifetime spent strapped down with student loans, mortgages, car loans, and consumer debt. This is modern-day indentured servitude.

There is always someone to pay and never enough time. We come to know life as a blur of deadlines, traffic jams, and fluorescent-lit checkout lines. We run on stress and caffeine, then soothe ourselves with doses of escapism—television, movies, Internet surfing.

All of this is continually punctuated by round-the-clock news and relentless advertising to convince us that we need to purchase things we wouldn't otherwise think about. We end up living for the future, dreaming of those occasional times when we will be unhooked from the corporate yoke for a vacation. And then there is retirement—namely, "Give us your youth and we will leave you with your old age"—if we make it that far.

Our collective success is measured mainly in terms of economic growth, despite the devastation of the natural world necessary to sustain that growth, which is like buying a house and ignoring the mortgage. Too many of us have lost the ability to live in the natural world— independent of electricity, plumbing, gasoline, industrial farming, and next-day delivery. We have forsaken ancient wisdom in favor of specialized knowledge and degrees. There is no longer time to reflect, time for ceremony, time to listen to the stories of the elders. We have become little machines running around doing mechanical things to keep the big machine running.

Some people call it consumerism, some call it the rat race. Very few call it healthy.

Perhaps you see yourself in the preceding scenario, and perhaps you don't. I know I didn't; after all, I lived an "alternative lifestyle." I was better than that, beyond that. I was more spiritually evolved, more socially conscious. Then I woke up. I saw that there was no escape— the virus had crept in everywhere, it infected everything. Yet I found a way out . . . .

My parents grew up in the Great Depression of the 1930s. There was no rat race then—the economy stood at a standstill. My mother tells me stories of growing up on a tiny hardscrabble immigrant farm with eleven other children. Some of them went to school only through eighth grade simply because there was no more money for school clothes. Their bag lunches often consisted of just lard on bread. My father's childhood in the city proved equally challenging—he and his family survived by converting their backyard to a garden and keeping rabbits and pigeons.

World War II pulled the nation out of the Depression, yet it didn't pull the self-reliant mentality out of my parents. The national economy had collapsed during the Depression, yet many family economies, such as my parents', were thriving. Mom and Dad still look fondly on their childhoods as times of personal richness, family closeness, and bounty.

After the war, many people wanted to blot the Depression years from their memories and ride the wave of the new affluence that was sweeping the country. Not my parents. My childhood consisted of lessons in frugality: "Reduce, reuse, and recycle" was more than a slogan for them. They taught me how to be happy and provide for many of my own needs so that I would not have to rely on money or consumer goods. To this day my mother still makes many of the things she uses, picks up castoff items from the curb, and shops at thrift stores and yard sales. She gathers wild nuts, berries, and greens, and gleans from farm fields what the harvesters leave behind. Her example has helped to form my concepts of sustenance and comfort.

My father's most important lesson to me has been that attitude is everything. If I think I am poor, I will be poor; if I think I am living in abundance, I will create abundance. The following story embraces my father's philosophy.

Not long ago, a wealthy man took his boy on a trip to the country to show him what it is like to be poor. They rented a room from what the man considered to be a poor farm family and spent a few days there. On the drive home, the man asked his son how he had enjoyed the trip.

"I had a great time," replied the son. "I learned a lot."

"Did you see what it's like to be poor?" asked the father.

The son replied, "I sure did!"

"Well then, tell me what you have learned," encouraged the father.

"Sure, Dad. We have one dog and one cat at home; I counted four dogs there, and I don't even think I saw all their cats. We have a lily pond that I can easily throw my ball across, and they have a creek that I followed all afternoon and I still couldn't find the end. At night our fancy patio lights go on; they have a thousand stars sparkling above them, and those stars make some of the neatest patterns! Our yard goes as far as the front gate; I think their fields and woods go all the way to the horizon! We have people who serve us; they seem happiest when they can serve others. We have to buy our food, and they grow their own. We have fences and alarm systems to protect us and our property, while they have neighbors and friends to protect them."

A silence followed—the father was at a loss for words.

After a moment, the son added, "Thank you, Dad, for showing me what poverty really is."

The Natural Economy

Through their example, my parents introduced me to the natural law of economics that has run the affairs of this world since its creation. It is the law by which all free-living things live—that the Earth Mother, the Mother of us all, cares for her children. We do not have to be obsessed with toiling or saving, sowing or reaping. The abundance is just there, and it keeps increasing on its own *if* we recognize it and live in balance with it. Life can then be a continual feast. That is why some native people call it the "gifting way."

This natural economy is based on giving. Life itself is seen as a gift, so life's needs are freely given. This view creates cooperation and sharing, which engenders feelings of belonging and being cared about. Thus a gift is given and received on two levels: from hand to hand, and from heart to heart. Giving creates trust and friendship—the foundations of thriving community and rich culture.

There is another law of economics. It was invented by people and is called the consumer economy. It is based on scarcity—the belief that there is a limited quantity of goods to go around, so people must compete for them. This belief further implies that goods will disappear unless they are hoarded, and that we must keep laboring to create more.

Competitiveness for limited resources creates self-centered, possessive, and aggressive people. Goods are shared by exchange rather than giving. The exchange is based on value, which is created by scarcity and demand. The exchange rate causes people to be cautious and calculating, even suspicious: "Is this worth the money they're asking?" "Do you think that car salesman is honest?"

Such attitudes isolate us from one another, both physically and emotionally. The more we exchange and the more we hoard, the more isolated we become, and the more our communities and cultures erode.

In the natural economy there is a vitality and abundance that is spontaneous and needs little organization or tending. Peace, happiness, and self-fulfillment are its gifts. The consumer economy can offer us only substitutes for those gifts, and of course they have to be purchased: "Eat this food and you will feel good." "Wear these clothes and you will look good." "Get this degree and you will be somebody who matters." "Buy this house and you will be the king of your own castle."

How to Get It Back

So many people I know are already feeling too isolated and mistrusting to come together with others and rejoin the natural economy. Many of us have become so out of touch with ourselves that we no longer know our natural inclinations; and even if we did, we have grown too passive to voice them. Clever advertising has conditioned us to use consumer goods and entertainment to fill the emptiness.

Even so, the yearning to live the way we are intended surfaces. Nearly every time we turn to our compulsions and addictions, it is an attempt to placate that unidentifiable yearning. All we know is that we need something more than what the consumer economy offers us; we just can't seem to get a grip on what that something more is.

Deep inside, we do know what it is. We crave the life of meaning that lies at the heart of the natural economy. We cannot help but crave it—we are organically programmed not only to function, but to thrive, in the natural economy. That is why it is able to give value and richness to so many aspects of life.

Awareness is the first step in virtually all healing; my reason for writing this is to share what I have learned in this first step, so that perhaps it might help you take yours. Then it will be possible to adopt new life goals based on the qualitative rather than the quantitative, so we can begin taking steps out of a life of riches and into an enriched life. We can forgo our dependence on the cash economy and join the interdependent circle of the natural economy.

My Road to Poverty

As strongly as my family background had rooted me in the natural economy, it still turned out that I needed to choose it consciously in order to
live it mindfully. That choosing began on my first flight from home, when
I attended a seminary to become a priest. I needed separation from my
family in order to find out who I was as an individual. I needed the
opportunity to experience on my own what materialism did and did not
hold for me.

An acolyte takes three vows on becoming a priest—poverty, chastity,
and obedience. I was not destined for the priesthood, in part because I
was called to a different sort of chastity and obedience than the church
had in mind. Yet I took a private vow of poverty, because I agreed in
principle, if not in practice, with the Church's philosophy of nonposses-
sion. I felt as though I was deciding to serve life in a greater sense,
rather than living my life focused on myself.

The vow I made caused some confusion among some of my friends.
When they heard *poverty* they envisioned homeless people, Third World
destitution, and religious ascetics sequestered in austere monasteries.

From my perspective, what I actually did was take a vow of abundance. By not letting money or possessions be the primary considerations
in the decisions I made, I opened myself to a broad range of possibilities.
I could more easily hear the voices guiding me. I had more time for
matters of the soul, for other people, and for the issues that mattered to
me. Most surprisingly, I came to realize that by not focusing on myself,
I actually had more time for myself. I had time to relax and just be, and
to take care of myself.

Now, that's prosperity! I quit worrying about how I was going to
make a living and instead started living. No longer was I anxious about
how I was going to support a family someday. I began to focus instead
on the growth and healing I needed to undergo in order to have a healthy
and prosperous family. I quit obsessing about the future—health care
costs, my children's college expenses, money for retirement—and strove
to live in the moment.

By not focusing on money, I felt myself growing richer than I ever imagined. Doors of opportunity began to open for me without the need of a degree, a high-powered position, or a silver spoon in my mouth. I learned how to partake in the benefits of society without selling my soul for them. I had the energy and centeredness to seek the personal bliss that a guru knows, without having to forsake everything and steal away to some isolated cave. In short, I learned how I could live fully without dying in the process.

Money: What Is It Good For?

Along with the evolution in my perspective on poverty, I changed my view of money. For all its mythologized glitz and glamour, money is quite simply a tool—no more and no less. Tools serve us well when we take care of them and know how to use them. When we have extra money, let us put it to work and not waste it. Perhaps we could give it to someone else who is striving to return to the gifting economy. Or maybe we could loan it out, just as we would a tool to a neighbor who needs it.

Perhaps the greatest gift I received on my road to poverty was the realization that real poverty is poverty of spirit. I looked around me and saw thousands of people classed as "poor" who were warm, dry, and clothed; who had three meals a day, entertainment centers, and cars. What was missing? If these people were poor, what were the people of Somalia and Bangladesh? Was the monk who chose a life of voluntary simplicity poor? What about the homesteader who relishes living without electricity and a sport-utility vehicle? And then there is the wealthy person who cannot seem to buy enough to quench her thirst; is she rich?

How Poverty Brings Riches

In the process of becoming "poor," I discovered something of phenomenal importance. It is not as though I had never before heard of it; it is not as though I didn't already believe in it. I had just never experienced it, so I did not know whether it could be true for me. It seemed to be something reserved only for good, just, and noble people.

This discovery came about because of the opening within me that my poverty created. It allowed me to reconnect with my heart of hearts—the center of my being where my intuition, senses, feelings, mind, and ancestral memories all joined together to guide me. Through trial and error I came to realize that when I followed my heart of hearts rather than just acting out of concern for my material welfare, those material needs were somehow also taken care of. In fact, I was often provided for better than when I placed material considerations first!

Listening to my heart of hearts gradually became the cornerstone of my lifestyle. What came to matter most was to honor all life and follow my vision—my reason for being. Over time, as I grew to trust the voice of my heart of hearts, my material needs took less and less energy and had less and less influence in my decision making. The transition went so smoothly that it hardly drew my attention. It was almost as though my physical needs were taking care of themselves.

Sometime later I grew curious about how this could be. I did not think about it as a child, because I naturally trusted in my parents' ways. Now, however, I came to realize that the natural economy seems to defy conventional wisdom.

The answer came one afternoon on a canoe trip, as I lazily drifted across a beaver pond. I realized that if I paddled upstream against the current I would need to expend quite a bit of energy, but if I paddled downstream the flow of the current could carry me. "Of course!" I exclaimed aloud. "If I am in alignment with the natural economy, I will be gifted; if I work against it, I will struggle!"

When things are meant to be, I realized, they just naturally fall into place, and my energy naturally complements their unfolding. They don't have to be forced. In fact, forcing something that is not intended to happen creates resistance. Working to overcome that resistance demands even more of my time, attention, and resources.

That did not mean that all I had to do was sit back and let things fall in my lap. I found out that I had to be an active player in my life—I had to have *passion*. When I believed in something, my whole being was involved in it, which greatly increased the odds that it would turn out well.

You have likely heard stories of people with money and secure jobs who let it all go to follow their bliss. They often found happiness, and to their surprise, some of them also found themselves better off financially. Yet most of them will tell you that their real gift was letting go of the fear that they would wake up one morning in their elder years exclaiming, "Why didn't I follow my bliss? Now I'll never know what could have been!"

Don't get me wrong—I'm not advocating that we all drop everything and go traipse off to la-la land. Being active players in our own unfoldings means that we proceed consciously and responsibly. It is then that we are provided for. One of those provisions is that if our plan A does not work, there is usually a plan B waiting in the wings. Another possibility is that we will discover that Plan A is just the preface to what is truly intended for us.

Along with passion we need *courage*. Even though we might be fools not to follow our bliss, it can still take tremendous courage to open the door and step out into the wind. In this culture, courage seems to be reserved for people we read about and people in the movies—those who are on grand adventures and doing exciting things with their lives.

If life itself is not a grand adventure, then what is? Is not the reason you picked up this book to help bring the spirit of adventure back into your life? If you were still paralyzed with fear, would you not right now be listening to your head and doing something more "productive"? What you are doing right now, this moment, takes courage.

Perhaps the main reason many of us have not known courage is because it has not been *encouraged*. Courage can be disruptive to the status quo because it leads to bliss. People in their bliss might lose the desire to conform. Without conformity the status quo cannot rely on masses of numbed, unadventurous workers to maintain itself.

Many people are helped with the courage to take those first steps back to the natural economy when they realize that if worse comes to worst, they can usually go back to the situation whence they came.

A Vision of Abundance

My dream is for all of us to be free to follow our inner voices and thus be able to share the unique beauty that we each hold. We will then nourish life, and nourish one another. We no longer need to trade away our time, our freedom, and our grandchildren's future for a handful of dollars and empty promises. It is time to reclaim the independence known to our ancestors and to help inspire the rest of wavering humanity to return to balance with the universal cycles and rhythms that govern our gentle Earth Mother. One person at a time, one step at a time, we can build a sustainable reality for our own profound enjoyment and for the benefit of all generations to come.

HEALING WITH MAGICK

JAMIE WOOD

I was born with magick careening through my veins. Gnarled trees and drops of dew possessed a beauty and enchantment that mundane, clumsy words fell short of describing, and defending and honoring Nature's spiritual essence and right to thrive unencumbered became a lifetime adventure.

In the beginning of my spiritual path, I wondered why no one else saw the majesty, depth, and yet simple magick in everyday life; why no one else saw themselves as able to create like Mother Nature. I was saddened without a human mirror for my worldview. And like many Pagans, I formed a kinship and trust with the natural world, discovering family everywhere I looked: in Mother Earth, Father Sun, Grandmother (or Sister) Moon, Grandfather Sky, Brother Wind, each and every animal.

My tree-hugging nature, coupled with my belief in everyone's powerfully creative force and spiritual responsibility, seemed disconnected from each other until I found Paganism. These beings of like mind also practiced their ability to use consciousness or magick as a means of focusing illimitable energy into a life of their choosing.

Finding a Pagan family is like a homecoming—the presence of support is exquisitely sweet, like a drop of water cooling a parched throat. Finally, someone else spoke the language of my heart and soul. Finally, I had someone with whom to celebrate the reverence for the seasons, the wonderment of life, and ourselves as Spirit, the great creators.

I combine the forces of Nature and focused intent to heal my mind, body, and soul. First I like to begin with a clearing of the slate, or preparation of the vessels of my mind and body to receive the unlimited abundance of light and love from the Universe. For me, cleansing begins with forgiveness as a means of making myself whole and clean. Once I am emptied of the victim mentality, I have a better understanding of myself as Divinity itself and am filled with a sense of peace and love. What is interesting is how little energy and how few tools it takes to foster forgiveness. It is merely a matter of remembering that there is nothing I am not, and ultimately there is only Light. We are here for a human experience, to live viscerally and bring heaven to earth.

Emptied of anger, unforgiveness, and low vibrational energy, I then turn to creating awareness of and paying attention to my gifts, the fertile ground for my talents and higher expressions of Spirit to grow and strengthen. In the magickal recipe at the end of this essay, carrots symbolize the fact that our talents and gifts may lie underneath the soil of our consciousness, deep within our subconscious. With focused intent we can cultivate our gifts and encourage them to grow. The roasted carrots recipe will help you discover the amazing talents and beauty waiting to spring forth into action.

Forgive Someone

Forgiving people does not mean that you excuse or condone their behavior. The reason to forgive is that resentment fosters anger, and anger corrodes the vessel that contains it. According to *Webster's New World Dictionary,* the word *forgive* means to "give up resentment against or the desire to punish; pardon; overlook an offense; cancel a debt." Thus the goal of forgiveness is to let go of hurts and move ahead with life—regardless of what people did to you, whether they did it to you once or maybe a few times. But every time you relive the incident, it is as if you do it to yourself again and again. Reliving painful events and situations brings toxins and other pollutants into your body. Your thoughts determine your health, both mental and physical. If you harbor and hold sadness in your heart long enough, it will eventually need to escape and find an outward expression, which can result in serious illness or, at the very least, restrained living.

Who has become the perpetrator now? You can forgive offenders and still choose not to reestablish a relationship with them. You need not become a doormat or allow them to hurt you again.

A lack of forgiveness gives others power over you. Withholding forgiveness and nursing resentment simply allows other people to have control over your well-being. It is always a mistake to let such negative emotions influence your living. Forgive, and you will be able to direct your life with positive thoughts and action.

To become a tolerant forgiver of major hurts, first practice forgiveness on small ones. Try the spell below on small slights or insults, especially those inflicted by strangers—someone who cut in line, a rude salesperson, and so on. Use these events as practice to prepare you for the tougher task of forgiving major hurts.

During the waning of the moon, light a black candle for the banishment of your resentment. Burn frankincense and myrrh incense. Write a letter on a piece of parchment paper to the person who hurt you. Express fully, clearly, and honestly how you feel and why that person's action hurt you and made you angry. Say whatever you want, using whatever language fully expresses how you feel—you will not be mailing this letter, so you do not have to censor yourself, either your anger or the depth of your sadness. Finish the letter with the bold declaration that you have forgiven him or her. Fold the letter and allow the wax from the candle to drip onto the fold, sealing it. As you do this, say,

> I now forgive and release,
> Embracing harmony and peace,
> From the pain I am free
> To live my life weightlessly.

Roasted Carrots

During the Wiccan holiday of the autumnal equinox, we find ourselves in the middle of the harvesting season, waiting and hoping for the results of an abundant year. Foods that are grown underground have special significance during the autumnal equinox. Taking cues from Mother Nature, Wiccans are invited by the Goddess and her consort to move inward, toward the depths of your being: to go underground like the carrot.

The new moon is symbolic of the darkness before creation, when all things are possible. The new moon that rises during the autumnal equinox often precedes the harvest full moon. Traditionally, Pagans acknowledge the harvest moon as the most powerful in helping us attain our needs and desires. Therefore it stands to reason that the new moon preceding the harvest moon is the most powerful time to excavate concealed or secret gifts.

We all have hidden talents; sometimes even our most significant ones are hidden. These abilities are important and beneficial because they represent our true selves. They exemplify all that we would love to share with our friends and family, but are afraid to because we fear ridicule, failure, or something more devious.

To draw out your special gift and the confidence to let it shine in the world, begin with a grounding rite. One way to do this is to envision yourself as a tree with roots extending to Mother Earth and branches reaching toward Father Sun. Bring in the warmth of the sun, then let its energy stretch out toward your toes and go down into the soil. When you feel centered, light a red candle and hold a clear crystal between your hands, saying,

> Goddess, grant me the strength to see the wisdom
> Of sharing the gift you have given me.
> Open my eyes to the confidence already in me to fulfill my destiny.
> Help me to erect a shield to protect my fragile self
> From words of doubt and ridicule.
> Turn my own words into empowering words of a proactive nature.

Remind me of the joy I found as a child, and help me to live it
every day.
I have a gift to bring to this world.
I have a unique talent no one else has.
I have the power to create the perfect space
For my authentic self to shine through.
I am now fulfilling my dream to . . . [fill in the blank].

Seal the spell by saying,

Do good unto all and no harm come to me,
By the will of my highest power,
This spell I cast three times three times three.
So mote it be.

1   pound carrots (8 large or 10 medium)
2½ tablespoons olive oil
2   teaspoons Chardonnay (or other dry white wine)
2   teaspoons white wine vinegar
1   tablespoon minced fresh parsley
1   tablespoon minced fresh tarragon
½   teaspoon minced fresh marjoram
     Salt and freshly ground black pepper to taste

Preheat the oven to 400°F. Peel the carrots and place in a baking dish.
Brush lightly with the oil. Roast for 10 to 15 minutes, or until golden
brown. Slice the carrots and place in a serving dish. Drizzle the wine
and vinegar over the carrots. Sprinkle on the fresh herbs (note that
complementary herbs such as dill or thyme may be substituted according to your taste). Season with salt and pepper to taste. Serves 4.

HOMEGROWN
COUGH SYRUP

MIKE SHORT

Here's a little recipe I've put together over the years because my lady wife is allergic to cane sugar in all its forms. Take two teaspoons every three to four hours. For a stomachache remedy, you can substitute a quarter cup of thinly sliced fresh ginger in place of the anise and cinnamon.

    2   cups water
    4 to 5 pods star anise
    1   cinnamon stick
    2   cups honey

Pour the water into a small saucepan. Measure and mark the depth of the water on the handle of a wooden spoon. Bring the water to a slow boil and then turn off the heat. Add the anise and cinnamon to the water; let stand for 15 to 20 minutes. Scoop out the anise and cinnamon. Bring the water back to a slow simmer. Add the honey and slowly reduce the volume over low heat until you have just the original 2 cups left. Do not let the honey mixture boil; it'll turn bitter faster than you might believe.

LOVE: STRAWBERRY MOUSSE ROMANCE INDUCER

Dorothy Morrison

Contrary to popular belief, men are born worriers when it comes to love and romance. They worry about finding it. They worry about keeping it. But most of all, they worry about losing it. I'd never given this much thought, however, until I was ripped from sound slumber early one morning by a loud banging noise—and it appeared to be coming from my front door.

The guy with the heavy hand turned out to be a friend of mine, and he was more than just a little upset. With busy schedules and separate agendas, it seemed that he and his wife were spending less and less time together. And the poor man was so worried that they were drifting apart, he was nearly in tears.

What he really wanted, of course, was some good old-fashioned romance and a little time alone with his wife. In fact, he'd already gone to the trouble to arrange it. The calendar was cleared, the babysitter was in place, and the flowers were on order. He'd even made plans to cook a scrumptious gourmet dinner. All he needed from me was the final shot in the arm—something to empower the romance he envisioned and make it an evening to remember.

Because his wife is very fond of strawberries—themselves a terrific romance booster—we settled on this incredibly magickal dessert. Prepared while visualizing romantic intentions and spoon-fed to your love in bed, it's something that no heart can possibly resist.

4	cups fresh strawberries, sliced
½	cup confectioners' sugar
1	teaspoon vanilla extract
1½	tablespoons unflavored gelatin
¼	cup granulated sugar
1½	cups heavy whipping cream, chilled
	Whole strawberries for garnish (optional)

Mix the sliced strawberries, confectioners' sugar, and vanilla extract together in a bowl, and let stand for 20 minutes. Hold your hands over the bowl and chant something like

Fruit of joy and pure romance
Meld with sugar to enhance
The feelings deep within our hearts—
The sort we once felt as sweethearts—
Blend well with love's vanilla bean
To break what has become routine
And return the stirrings of devotion
Romance, love, and true emotion
To our bodies, minds, and hearts
Give our love a fresh new start.

Strain the fruit, reserving the juices, and puree the fruit in the blender. Place the puree in a mixing bowl and set aside. Transfer the juices to a small saucepan and add the gelatin. Let stand for 5 minutes, then stir constantly over low heat until the gelatin has dissolved completely. Add the juice mixture to the puree, and blend with a whisk while chanting something like

> Gelatin, I conjure you
> To set the spell of love that's true
> Together with love's precious fruit
> To bring us romance, absolute.

Place the mixture in the refrigerator for several hours, until it begins to set. Combine the granulated sugar with the cream, and beat until it stands in peaks. Set aside 1 cup of the whipped cream, and fold the rest into the partially set strawberry mixture, saying something like

> As I add you, sweetened cream,
> Into this spell, your gifts now stream
> Softening hearts and blending pleasure
> Endlessly within this treasure
> Cast for hearts which beat as one
> As I will, this spell is spun

Pour the strawberry mousse into parfait glasses or champagne flutes, and garnish with whipped cream and a whole strawberry, if desired. Chill until ready to serve, up to 1 day.

LOVE, PAGAN STYLE

SELENE SILVERWIND

When I cast a love spell to find my ideal mate six and a half years ago, I had a long list of qualities I was looking for. Pagan wasn't among them. Understanding and tolerance of my faith was the most I asked for. Then the Gods brought me the one who is now my fiancé, and I learned that I truly did need to be with someone who shared my faith.

Of course, I'm not saying this is true for everyone. I know many Pagans whose spouses or significant others are not Pagan and who have wonderful, successful relationships, but I've had several unsuccessful relationships with non-Pagans and now realize that a Pagan is the only option for me. Loving a fellow Pagan has helped my Paganism evolve in new directions, and being Pagan gives us the tools and skills necessary to keep our relationship flourishing. Sharing our faith has created yet another bond for our relationship and deepened the connection we share with each other and our religion. During the course of our six years together, we've celebrated many Sabbats, performed many spells, and survived several trials and complications. None of that would have been possible without our shared faith.

The first Sabbat we celebrated together was Samhain (Hallows). It was a powerful evening for both of us, but not a sad one. Not only were we joyously embarking on a new relationship, but that night marks my parents' anniversary—a positive sign for our future if ever there was one. I knew shortly after we started dating that he was the one. He was everything I had asked for, and many things I had not known to ask for. He had adopted the Wiccan faith shortly before we started dating, and it became another level on which we could learn, grow, and connect.

As our relationship grew, so did our experience of our faith. We were honored to be the May queen and king on our first Beltane (May Eve) together. During the ritual, we crowned each other with wreaths I had made years before, offered each other bawdy cookies to ensure a lustful eve, and then led the maypole dance. By the time we got home, we were fully engrossed in our roles as king and queen of the May and finished the evening with a rousing rendition of the Great Rite. To this day, our crowns hang on our bedposts as a reminder of that night and the awesome power of the God and Goddess when they infused us with their spirits that night.

The following Lammas (August 1), when my circle hosted a large campout, I realized just how deeply my relationship with a Pagan had affected my Paganism. By then my lover had joined my circle, and we both looked forward to the trip. I had brought a non-Pagan boyfriend with me in the past, but had felt restricted by the need to sit by his side and explain everything to him. This was my first trip with a Pagan I was romantically involved with. Being there with someone who shared my beliefs and reverence for nature freed me to let myself be seduced by the siren song of the drum circle as I danced around the fire. It freed me to become one with Nature as we hiked to the top of the nearby mountain peak and climbed atop a boulder to watch an eagle soar over-head. As we soaked in the sound of drums drifting up from the campground below, I was overcome by the magick of the moment and knew my lover was reveling in the same deep sensation of being caressed by the God and Goddess. I could never have explained myself to a non-Pagan lover, but my Pagan lover didn't require any explanation. He already knew.

The Goddess has been with us throughout our relationship, and we look to her for guidance. The God has joined her in leading us more than once, and together my lover and I do our best to honor them for the example they give us as the Goddess and her consort, the Horned God and his bride. We look to them not only in times of joy, but in times of trouble. Over the course of the past six years we've suffered through challenges to our relationship and our health, but we have always been able to call on the Goddess and God for help when we are in need. We ask them to speed healing to the places it is needed and call on our network of Pagan friends to help us find what we seek. When we need only inner healing, we release our sorrow to the gods, and they accept it openly. They have never turned their backs on us, and we are grateful for that. With a Pagan as my mate, I know that he will always understand when I need to turn to the Goddess for more help.

Now, as we prepare to join ourselves in marriage, we look more and more to the Goddess and God as we seek a way to honor them through our handfasting ceremony and our marriage. We look forward to declaring our commitment to each other before them. They have helped us strengthen our relationship and build a firm foundation. We know they will always be there to help us along the winding road of life.

I trust that my lover and I will always share our love and our Paganism. Our lives will change, and as they do, our faith will help keep our bond strong. Through our love for each other and our experience of the world together, our beliefs will grow and deepen to levels not yet knowable. We will remain forever touched by the Goddess and God as they guide us in our love and our lives. It promises to be an interesting, arousing, educational voyage. I could not wish to have anyone else but my lover by my side as I travel it. Our faith is as much a part of our bond as our love and dedication to each other.

LUCK: GOLDEN SUNSHINE *SCHMARN*

JANINA RENÉE

An African saying teaches that "A good day starts in the morning," and a German saying goes, "The morning hour has gold in its mouth" (*Morgen Stund hat Gold im Mund*). Both emphasize that we have to make our own luck by getting up early and getting things done. To activate some golden morning luck, make some *schmarn* for breakfast. It is a German specialty made with a pancakelike batter, but cooked the way you would make scrambled eggs; it will get your day off to an auspicious start. This "sunshine *schmarn*" is my own adaptation of the traditional dish. You could serve it along with poached eggs and sausage.

1	cup whole wheat flour
1	teaspoon baking powder
½	teaspoon baking soda
½	teaspoon salt
4	large eggs

8   ounces flavored yogurt (especially peach, lemon, or tropical
      fruit)
¼   cup milk
1   cup crushed pineapple or pineapple tidbits, drained
½   cup sweetened coconut flakes
2   tablespoons cooking oil (such as canola oil)

In a medium bowl, mix the whole wheat flour, baking powder, baking soda, and salt. In a larger bowl, beat the eggs, then mix with the flavored yogurt and milk. Blend the dry ingredients into the egg mixture. Stir in the drained pineapple and coconut.

Heat a large griddle, then add the oil. When the griddle is hot enough for pancakes, pour on the batter; stir it around as you would when making scrambled eggs. Fry it until it has a crumbly texture and a nice golden color. Serves 4.

TAROT FOR HEALING

CHRISTINE JETTE

*There is a test to find if your mission on earth
is finished. If you're alive, it isn't.*

—Richard Bach—

Using the tarot cards for healing offers a way to step outside ordinary consciousness and discover an intuitive connection among you, the healer within, and a universal healing force. The cards' images are filled with healing energies that direct you toward wholeness. Wellness is body, mind, and spirit in balance. Tarot reveals areas that are out of balance and gives advice on the best ways to restore order.

A word to the wise: Using the tarot for healing complements, but does not replace, standard medical care. Tarot work supplements professional care, bringing the unconscious mind into harmony with the physical self to assist the healing process. They can help you understand the reasons behind disease, but their use does not diagnose, treat, or prescribe; and this layout is not intended for primary medical intervention. If you have symptoms, contact your health professional of choice before proceeding.

The Four Levels of Illness and Healing

In illness and healing, there is no separation of body, emotion, mind, and spirit. It is impossible to be ill without all four levels of existence being affected. It is likewise impossible to heal without attending to these same four levels of being.

Try this spread when feeling out of ease with any areas of your life. It will pinpoint situations that are no longer useful to you. If you like a card, it shows where you are strong. If a card is challenging, it will either be a clear depiction of the area in which you are wounded or show you what you need to release for healing to occur.

If you have a specific health concern, concentrate on it while shuffling the cards and relate the information of the spread directly to your concern. The layout roughly follows the alignment of our chakras, or energy centers along the spine.

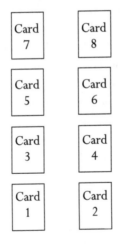

Card 1: The physical plane of illness. What is your body trying to tell you? What messages for needed changes in lifestyle or thinking do physical symptoms carry?

Card 2: The physical plane of healing. This card gives advice about card 1. What action can you take on your own behalf to support the healing process on the physical level?

Card 3: The emotional plane of illness. Card 3 illuminates the role of your emotions in "dis-ease." What messages of wounding do your emotions convey? Fear frequently shows up here.

Card 4: The emotional plane of healing. This card gives advice about card 3. What action can you take on your own behalf to support the healing process on the emotional level?

Card 5: The psychological plane of illness. The card that appears here shows the way your mind works. It describes how thought processes may interfere with health and wellness.

Card 6: The psychological plane of healing. This card gives advice about card 5. What action can you take on your own behalf to support the healing process on the psychological level?

Card 7: The spiritual plane of illness. Areas of life that interfere with spiritual well-being appear here. Ask these questions: Are you being true to your authentic self? Have you set up the wrong life for you?

Card 8: The spiritual plane of healing. This card gives advice about card 7. What action can you take on your own behalf to support the healing process on the spiritual level? Many times, cards indicating creativity, developing intuition, changing jobs, ending worn-out relationships, saying no, or nurturing self or the need to play will show up here.

Powerful healing does not emerge from laboratories and technological advances. Instead, it is the use of self, in a loving and compassionate way, that provides our most powerful tool for healing. Health and happiness are "in the cards" for *you*.

ABOUT THE CONTRIBUTORS

Margot Adler started studying the Craft in 1971. She became a priestess in the Gardnerian tradition in 1973 and led a Gardnerian coven for many years. Her current practice is eclectic Wicca and Paganism. She is the author of *Drawing Down the Moon* (Penguin, 1997), the classic study of Neopaganism and Goddess spirituality, first published in 1979 and revised in 1986. She has also written *Heretic's Heart,* a political and spiritual memoir focusing on the 1960s and 1970s. She gives lectures and workshops on Paganism, ritual, and song. In her mundane life she has been a public-radio correspondent and producer for more than thirty-five years. At present, she is the New York correspondent for National Public Radio's national news shows: *All Things Considered, Morning Edition,* and *Weekend Edition.* She is also the host of *Justice Talking,* a debate show that airs on about a hundred stations and focuses on the U.S. Constitution. Produced by the Annenberg Public Policy Center, it is recorded at the National Constitution Center in Philadelphia.

Ardy has been active in the west-central Florida Pagan community for umpteen years now (since shots were fired at Lothlorien all those years ago, anyway). She has been high priestess of Dragonwood Circle for fourteen years, and she's a sixty-one-year-old, postmenopausal crone. If you want something more specific, you'll have to ask. Many people have come into her circle since those early days, and many have moved on to other groups or other states. Ardy and her circle are eclectic, with a Wiccan foundation. They hold regular Sabbat celebrations at which children are welcome.

Branwen has a Ph.D. in anthropology and several published works. Magickally she has been involved in Pagan and Witchcraft activities for more than two decades. Her experience began with studies of shamanism but soon moved toward Witchcraft. At present, she is an eclectic solitary Witch and a priestess of Oshun (from the West African Orisa tradition). She is also the facilitator for Branwen's Cauldron of Light and Magickware shop. Visit both online at www.branwenscauldron.com and www.magickware.com.

Cinnamon Moon is a medicine woman, minister, and author of *A Medicine Woman Speaks* (New Page Books, 2001). She has also served as a spiritual adviser to both private and commercial clients worldwide for more than thirty-five years. For more info, visit www.keen.com/memberpub/homepage.asp?user= CinnamonMoon.

Phyllis Curott is a social and spiritual activist and has been an attorney and Wiccan priestess for more than twenty years. She is also the author of the best-selling *Book of Shadows: A Modern Woman's Journey into the Wisdom of Witchcraft and the Magic of the Goddess* (Broadway Books, 1998), of *Witch Crafting: A Spiritual Guide to Making Magic* (Broadway Books, 2001), and of *The Love Spell* (Gotham, 2005). High Priestess Curott is the founder of the Temple of Ara. She addressed the Parliament of the World's Religions as a keynote speaker, along with the Dalai Lama, and was honored by *Jane* magazine as one of the Ten Greatest Women of 1998. High Priestess Curott lectures and teaches internationally. Visit her at www.phylliscurott.com.

Siryn Dolphinsong has been involved with Paganism her whole life. She is a thirty-eight-year-old eclectic Witch who draws from Yoruba as well as Celtic and folk traditions; her beliefs include a condemnation of censorship or judgment by any human and an oath of honesty. Rather, she says, the answer to all religious ignorance is freedom and education. To Siryn, networking and meeting new Pagans is the greatest way to find the perfect family. In 2003 Siryn opened Bio-Buzz Botanica, a metaphysical store in Albany, Georgia, with life partner, Stephen. There, Siryn holds regular workshops and discussion groups.

Mama Doyi-Astarte is initiated into a coven and has joined a sister tribal clan. She does everything possible to serve the community, including working with Pagan Nights Out (PNOs), Knoxville Area Pagans and Wiccans (KAPOW), gatherings, and open circles. She is currently the chairperson of the largest networking group in the Knoxville area, KAPOW, and the list owner for the local Pagan political discussion group.

Jennie Dunham has been a practicing Pagan since 1986. She is a literary agent who works with many New Age and Pagan authors. She lives in New York. On October 18, 2003, she gave birth to her son, Edward.

Earthwizard has been a Wiccan for more than three decades. Initiated by Doreen Valiente, he has at many points walked as a cunning man and *seanachai* (tale bearer of the old ways), and as poet, artist, and scholar of ancient traditions. Earthwizard believes strongly in the power and magick of poetry. He has followed the bardic track in realms of lore, legend, and myth: the primal songs of humanity. Additionally, he believes that we are, one and all, children of the moon, dark riders of eternity in love with the old ways of the Earth. As a poet, he measures the music of time in verses of delight and promise: the gift of the blessed Lady and Lord of all life. Visit him online at www.earthwisdom.info.

Katelan V. Foisy graduated from the Pratt Institute with a B.A. in illustration. Her work has been seen in various galleries in the United States and the United Kingdom. Katelan currently works as a freelance illustrator in New York. She is working on a deck of tarot cards that she wishes to publish in the future. For more info and to see her work, go to www.altpick.com/katelanv or email katelanv@verizon.net.

Rev. Alicia L. Folberth/HalfWolf is the high priestess and president of the Panthean Temple, formerly known as the Pagan Community Church, which was founded in 1995. She is the founder of the Inner Court of the church, Ceffylwen, and its new tradition, Panthean. She is also the initiator and a cofounder of the Pagan Interfaith Council. It is her conviction that the time has come for Pagan religions to claim their rights alongside mainstream faiths, and she has taken these first steps in creating organizations to establish Paganism and its worship in both the legal and the public eye. She is also active within the Department of Corrections, spiritually mentoring several Wiccan inmates. Visit www.pagan-communitychurch.org.

Rev. Selena Fox is senior minister and high priestess of Circle Sanctuary, a Wiccan church, resource center, and nature preserve with a worldwide ecospirituality ministry that includes networking, publishing, education, environmental preservation, counseling, event sponsorship, and other work. For more than twenty-five years, Rev. Fox has served as one of the elders, religious freedom activists, and public media spokespersons for the Wiccan religion, Paganism, and ecospirituality. Rev. Fox's professional life also includes being a guest speaker at colleges, civic groups, and wellness centers internationally. Her writings and photographs on spirituality, psychology, herbology, folkways, genealogy, and other topics have been published in a variety of books and periodicals as well as on the Internet. Visit her website at www.circlesanctuary.org.

Rowan Hall is the coauthor with Patricia Telesco of *Animal Spirit* (New Page Books, 2002). She is a wildlife biologist who has been an active member of the East Coast Pagan community for more than a decade, offering her services as a guardian, medical coordinator, and speaker at a wide variety of festivals and gatherings.

Bonnie Jean Hamilton is a Wiccan priestess with years of experience creating and leading rituals and ceremonies with an openness to all religions and walks of life, as she believes that all paths hold truth. She is a lifelong friend of the star people and has studied various metaphysical subjects, including energy manipulation, one of the basic foundations of this reality and others. A mother of two beautiful girls, she is married to her best friend of thirteen years. She has earned an associate's degree in arts and sciences and a bachelor's degree in cultural anthropology from the College of William & Mary. Her first book, *Invitation to the Self,* is forthcoming. Visit her at www.moonbeamproductions.com.

Jesse Wolf Hardin is an acclaimed teacher of Earth-centered spirituality, living seven river crossings from a road in an ancient place of power. He is most recently the author of *Kindred Spirits: Sacred Earth Wisdom* (Swan-Raven, 2001). Wolf and Loba share the riverside sanctuary where he offers men's quests and intuitive counsel, and she hosts women for quests, wild-foods gathering, and special resident internships. To host Wolf for university or conference presentations, or for info on their many books and programs, contact the Earthen Spirituality Project, P.O. Box 820, Reserve, NM 87830, or visit them online at www.earthenspirituality.org.

Ambrose Hawk was raised by a mystically experienced father who drew spiritual ideas from Cherokee and global beliefs. Ambrose first became active as a "consulting wizard" in the 1960s. Ironically, he also received formal theological training at the Pontifical Institute at the Catholic University of America, where he realized Christians can, indeed, be wizards. Ambrose has been active as a tarot reader, astrologer, and scryer. He is the independent researcher for A Mystickal Grove for its "Christian Earth Spirituality" page. He is the author of *Exploring Scrying* (New Page Books, 2001), and under his mundane name he has published about ninety poems and had a short career as a folksinger. He has returned to his Arkansas Ozarks with his beloved Jade and their pride of rescued cats.

Christine Jette (pronounced "Jetty") is a registered nurse and holds a B.A. degree in psychology. She is a therapeutic touch practitioner, member of the American Holistic Nurses Association, freelance technical writer, and nonfiction author. Her books include *Tarot Shadow Work* (Llewellyn, 2000), *Tarot for the Healing Heart* (Llewellyn, 2001), *Tarot for All Seasons* (Llewellyn, 2001), and *Professional Tarot* (Llewellyn, 2003). Christine lives in Cincinnati with her husband and three cats. Visit her on the Web at www.findingthemuse.com.

Lady Willow, cofounder of the OakNstone path, is an ordained interfaith minister. She is minister to the Gateway to the Sacred interfaith fellowship and High Mother priestess of the Coven of the Sacred Stone People. She is also a wife, mother of three daughters, licensed nurse and holistic practitioner, business owner, and artist. Her interests include tarot, natural healing, aromatherapy, travel, arts and crafts, and more. A perpetual student, she loves books and networking with people from all walks of life. Visit her at www.sacredoaks.org.

Judith Lewis is a high priestess, elder, and Witch with more than fifteen years' experience in studying and practicing the Craft. She has been teaching and running a coven for much of that time and uses her free time to run her online shop, experiment with incense, and create aromatherapy blends. She is, as all women seem to be, in the middle of writing her book. You can shop online with her at www.newmoonoccult shop.com.

Christena Linka works as a professional psychic with her psychic husband, Peter. Christena has studied the Craft since the early 1960s and is the founder of Deerglade, an eclectic Wiccan coven in Ontario, Canada. You can read about the coven and reach her at www.deerglade.com.

Loba is a priestess of sacrament and delight, presenting at Pagan and women's events and writing for various magazines. She hosts women for wilderness quests, wild-foods gathering weekends, resident apprenticeships, and the annual Wild Women's Gathering (write for dates). Contact the Sweet Medicine Women's Center and Earthen Spirituality Project, P.O. Box 820, Reserve, NM 87830, or visit www.earthenspirituality.org.

Kristin Madden is an author and homeschooling mom who was raised in a Pagan home. Her current books are *Shamanic Guide to Death and Dying* (Llewellyn, 1999), *Pagan Parenting* (Spilled Candy, 2004), *Mabon: Celebrating the Autumn Equinox* (Llewellyn, 2002), *The Book of Shamanic Healing* (Llewellyn, 2002), and *Pagan Homeschooling* (Spilled Candy, 2002). Kristin is a shamanic deathwalker, a healer, and a Druid in the Order of Bards, Ovates, and Druids. She is both faculty and board member for the Ardantane Project, a nonprofit organization dedicated to creating a Wiccan/Pagan seminary. She directs Ardantane's school of shamanic studies; serves on the board of directors of Silver Moon Health Services, a Pagan-sponsored nonprofit corporation; and offers workshops and interviews regularly. Visit her at www.kristinmadden.com.

Carl McColman practices an inclusive and postmodern form of Celtic mysticism. His books include *Before You Cast a Spell* (New Page Books, 2003), and *The Complete Idiot's Guide to Paganism* (Alpha, 2002). He lives in Stone Mountain, Georgia, with his wife, stepdaughter, and four cats, and is actively involved in community-building projects. You can visit him online at www.carlmccolman.com.

Dorothy Morrison has garnered numerous awards for her writing, including 1999 and 2000 COVR Visionary awards. Morrison's works include *The Craft* (Llewellyn, 2001), *The Craft Companion* (Llewellyn, 2001), *Bud, Blossom & Leaf* (Llewellyn, 2001), *Yule* (Llewellyn, 2000), *The Whimsical Tarot* (U.S. Games Systems, 2001), *Everyday Tarot Magic* (Llewellyn, 2002), and *Everyday Moon Magic* (Llewellyn, 2003). Dorothy currently lives in New England with her husband, Mark, and her black lab, Sadie Mae. A third-degree Wiccan high priestess in the Georgian tradition, she founded the Coven of the Crystal Garden in 1986 and spent many years teaching the Craft to students in eight states and Australia. Dubbed by *Publishers Weekly* "a witch to watch," she maintains a vigorous tour schedule and is ensconced in studies of the RavenMyst Circle tradition. Swing by www.dorothymorrison.com to learn all about her books and travels, as well as the projects she's supporting.

Ann Moura began writing about her heritage as a Green Witch after her mother passed away, combining the lessons she learned from her Brazilian mother and her grandmother of Celtic-Iberian descent. Besides this firm foundation, Ann holds both B.A. and M.A. degrees in history. Her books, available through the publisher and found at most bookstores, are *Green Witchcraft*, 3 vols. (Llewellyn, 1996), *Green Magic: The Sacred Connection to Nature* (Llewellyn, 2002), *Grimoire for the Green Witch: A Complete Book of Shadows* (Llewellyn, 2003), *Tarot for the Green Witch* (Llewellyn, 2003), *Witchcraft: An Alternative Path* (Llewellyn, 2003), and *Origins of Modern Witchcraft: The Evolution of a World Religion* (Llewellyn, 2000). Her books and more information can be found online at www.annmourasgarden.com.

Precious Nielsen is a medicine woman who began her training in her youngest days and studied under several teachers for more than thirty years. She teaches ancient Earth-based healing traditions and shamanism, and is an artist. She has degrees in nursing and religious studies and is a licensed reverend. Precious has four sons and three cats and lives quietly in Florida with her husband.

Ashleen O'Gaea lives in Pima County, Arizona, with her husband of thirty years, Canyondancer; a lovable Aussie-chow-idiot mutt called Barleycorn; and cats Hal, Bette, and Milo. She and 'Dancer have been public advocates for Wicca since 1986 and are among the founders of the Tucson Area Wiccan-Pagan Network (TAWN). They developed the Adventure tradition of Wicca and led its first coven, Campsight. O'Gaea's first work, *The Family Wicca Book* (Llewellyn), was published in 1993; she's also the author of *Raising Witches* (New Page Books, 2002) and *In the Service of Life* (Citadel, 2003), along with two volumes of *Celebrating the Seasons of Life* (New Page Books, 2004). In addition to being an active member of TAWN, she's the senior corresponding priestess for Mother Earth Ministries-ATC, a Neopagan prison ministry based in Tucson. Contact her through www.adventurewicca.com.

Laura Perry is a naturopath and author of *Ancient Spellcraft* (New Page Books, 2001) and *The Wiccan Wellness Book* (New Page Books, 2003). Laura also works as executive director of Healing Cove, Inc., a nonprofit wellness center dedicated to improving lives in northern Georgia through services, education, and outreach. Learn more about her work and writings at www.lauraperry.com.

Janina Renée is a scholar of material culture, folklore, mythology, ancient religion, psychology, medical anthropology, history, literature, and the cultural context and subject position of Asperger's syndrome and high-functioning autism. She is also the author of *Tarot Spells* (Llewellyn, 2000), *Playful Magic* (Llewellyn, 1994), *Tarot: Your Everyday Guide* (Llewellyn, 2000), *Tarot for a New Generation* (Llewellyn, 2001), and *By Candlelight: Rites for Celebration, Blessing & Prayer* (Llewellyn, 2004). You can order her books at www.llewellyn.com.

Bev Richardson is a Gardnerian who studied under Gerald Gardner himself, and the owner-operator of a natural-spiritual sanctuary in Ireland known as Castle Pook. He is among a unique breed of bards who is teaching this tradition by word and deed wherever he travels. Learn more about him and Castle Pook at www.paganireland.com.

Shae Moyers Rightmire, D.Div., is an ordained minister, psychic, and spiritual catalyst in private practice in the Chicago and Kansas City, Missouri, areas. Shae is a Magdalene high priestess, creator of The Calling priestess process (a psychospiritual empowerment program for women), and founder of Soul-Path, an online spiritual community. Bringing practicality to spirituality, for fifteen years Shae has been facilitating priestess circles, retreats, and workshops in which she creates a safe, nurturing space for profound personal transformation. Please contact her for more information on how you can host Shae to facilitate in your area: visit www.soulpath.org or email revshae@soulpath.org.

Mike Short started down the Pagan path in earnest as a Gardnerian. Since then he has gathered bits of Scandinavian and Native American beliefs to supplement basic Celtic Paganism. His only "complaint" about the path is that nobody warned him that somewhere along the line the word *priest* would be etherically tattooed on his forehead. Mike is currently the husband of Robin Wood, a friend of Skyia, and a slave to two cats. He consults as a technical trainer for computer diagnostic software and travels the world (England, Germany, and Sweden) to explain the folly of ignoring U.S. Environmental Protection Agency and European Environment Agency regulations.

Selene Silverwind is the author of *Magic for Lovers* (The Crossing Press, 2004), *The Everything Paganism Book* (Adams Media, 2004), the inspirational romance *Once upon a Beltane Eve* (Spilled Candy, 2001), and the novel *Field of Jonquils* (Spilled Candy, 2005). She lives in Los Angeles, where she is studying for an M.A. in English and creative writing. To learn more about her or her books, visit www.selenesilverwind.com.

Marian Singer is an eclectic solitary Pagan of twenty years' practice. She has recently begun writing New Age books, including *Everything Wicca and Witchcraft* (Adams Media, 2002), *Magick for the Wild Woman* (Adams Media, 2004), *Dancing the Fire* (Citadel, 2005), and *Candlelit Recipes for Magick* (Citadel, forthcoming). Marian considers herself a playful Pagan. She lives in upstate New York with her family and copious animal companions.

Tamarack Song's earliest memories are of the wild asparagus and daisies that grew around a prairie house, and of how his mother would use them to nourish both bodies and souls. She would combine her wild-foraged fare with the perfectly good discards of farmers and retailers to create hearty meals and luscious desserts. She learned these ways from her Native American mother, who could make beautiful and useful clothing from flour sacks. Together they taught him how to meet needs with hand and heart rather than by selling one's self for money. In order to help others learn sustaining, spirit-enriching ways to live, Tamarack is sharing his family heritage through his writings and through the Teaching Drum Outdoor School, which you can visit at www.teachingdrum.org.

Starhawk is one of the most respected voices in modern Goddess religion and Earth-based spirituality. She is the author or coauthor of ten books, including the timeless classics *The Spiral Dance* (HarperSanFrancisco, 1999 [orig. 1979]) and *The Fifth Sacred Thing* (Bantam, 1993). Her latest book is *The Earth Path* (HarperSanFrancisco, 2004). Starhawk is a veteran of progressive movements and deeply committed to bringing the techniques and creative power of spirituality to political activism. She travels internationally teaching magick, the tools of ritual, and the skills of activism. Visit her at www.starhawk.org.

Patricia Telesco is a mother of three, wife, chief human to five pets, and full-time author of more than fifty books. These include the best-selling *Goddess in My Pocket* (HarperSanFrancisco, 1998), *How to Be a Wicked Witch* (Fireside, 2001), *A Kitchen Witch's Cookbook* (Llewellyn, 1998), *Your Book of Shadows* (Citadel, 1999), *Spinning Spells, Weaving Wonders* (The Crossing Press, 1996), and *A Little Book of Mirror Magick* (The Crossing Press, 2003). She is a self-trained Wiccan, but she later received initiation into the Strega tradition of Italy, which gives form and fullness to the folk magick Patricia practices. She travels frequently to give lectures and workshops around the United States. You can visit her online at www.loresinger.com.

TerriLyn is a high priestess and clan mother for two clans. She raises dogs and writes. She began her journey with the death of a friend in 1991, first exploring Native American teachings and then the Craft a few years later. She continues to enjoy working with covens, dogs, teaching, writing, and the peace of a quiet house now that her sons are grown.

Gail Wood has been a Witch and Wiccan priestess for twenty years, practicing a shamanic path honoring the dark moon. She is a ritual leader, Reiki master, tarot reader, and teacher. Part of her ministry is working with incarcerated Pagans. She recently joined a coven in the RavenMyst Circle tradition and is enjoying being a student once again.

Jamie Wood, Dancing Butterfly Who Soars on the Wind, is a tree-hugging, dirt-worshipping Pagan who wildly celebrates the elementals at play in the world. She teaches, writes, and lives her life to share her beliefs and passions that we all create the life of our choosing and that magick is as natural and beautiful as a blade of grass. Jamie has coauthored *The Wicca Cookbook: Recipes, Ritual, and Lore* (Celestial Arts, 2000), and authored *The Teen Spell Book: Magick for Young Witches* (Celestial Arts, 2001), *The Wicca Herbal: Recipes, Magick, and Abundance* (Celestial Arts, 2003), and *The Enchanted Diary* (Celestial Arts, 2005). Visit her at www.jamiewood.com.

Oberon Zell-Ravenheart has been active in the Pagan community for more than forty years. He cofounded the Church of All Worlds in 1962. First to apply the terms *Pagan* and *Neopagan* to the newly emerging nature religions of the 1960s, and through his publication of the legendary journal, *Green Egg* (1968–1976; 1988–1996), Oberon has been instrumental in the coalescence of the modern Pagan movement. In 1970, he formulated and published the theology of deep ecology that has become known as the Gaia Thesis. Oberon is the primary artist of the Mythic Images collection, producing museum-quality replicas and original altar figurines. The centerpiece of this collection is his revelatory sculpture *The Millennial Gaia*. His first book is *Grimoire for the Apprentice Wizard* (New Page Books, 2004). Oberon lives with his extended family, the Ravenhearts, in Sonoma County, California. Learn more at www.mythicimages.com.

INDEX OF CONTRIBUTORS